Leaning into the Presence of the Lord

35 MEDITATIONS FOR CHALLENGING TIMES

Sue LeBoutillier

Copyright ©2025 by Sue LeBoutillier

All rights reserved.

No portion of this book may be reproduced in any form without written permission from the publisher or author, except as permitted by U.S. copyright law.

Unless otherwise noted, Scripture quotations are from The ESV® Bible (The Holy Bible, English Standard Version®), © 2001 by Crossway, a publishing ministry of Good News Publishers. Used by permission. All rights reserved."

Scripture quotations marked NIV84 are taken from the Holy Bible, New International Version®, NIV®. Copyright ©1973, 1978, 1984 by Biblica, Inc.™ Used by permission of Zondervan. All rights reserved worldwide. www.zondervan.com The "NIV" and "New International Version" are trademarks registered in the United States Patent and Trademark Office by Biblica, Inc.™

No portion of this book may be reproduced in any form without written permission from the publisher or author, except as permitted by U.S. copyright law.

Contents

	Introduction	1
1.	Leaning into the Lord	9
2.	A Summer Sabbatical	13
3.	Saturated in the Word	16
4.	Unexpected Paths	20
5.	Secret Clubs	24
6.	Under Construction	28
7.	Burger Season	33
8.	No Longer Sad	38
9.	Ebenezer	42
10.	When Life Leaves You Flattened	46
11.	It Won't Always be this Way	50

12.	Perplexing Decisions	55
13.	Don't Worry About Anything	59
14.	Stepping or Stopping?	64
15.	Smoke & Ashes	69
16.	How is Your Hearing?	73
17.	Strength to Strength	78
18.	Grace	83
19.	Planted on Purpose	86
20.	Perspective	90
21.	God's Hidden Hand	94
22.	A New Position	98
23.	Mixed Signals	102
24.	At Just the Right Time	106
25.	Factory Reset	109
26.	Why Not Me?	112
27.	The Power of Boredom	115
28.	Incremental Healing	118
29.	Yet, I Will Rejoice	122
30.	Distant	126
31.	Come Away	129

32.	Give thanks in all Circumstances?	132
33.	A Light has Dawned	135
34.	A Catalog of Empathy	139
35.	A Great Time for Friends	142
36.	Photo Album	147
37.	About the Author	149

Introduction

It's not unusual for people to sail through life minding their own business, enjoying their days and tallying up their years — until something unexpected happens. When it does, the normal rhythm of life is dramatically altered.

This happened to Moses in Exodus chapter 3. Sure, Moses had quite a dramatic young adult life, but since living in Midian he had been enjoying his days and tallying up his years — all 80 of them. But one day God came along and changed everything by giving him an assignment from a bush that wouldn't stop burning. Moses was to return to Egypt and tell Pharoah to let God's people go. Moses wasn't sure he was up for this task and told God so a few times.

This also happened to me earlier this year when I received a diagnosis of aggressive breast cancer. Suddenly my normal rhythm of life — enjoying my days and tallying my years — changed significantly. I also wasn't sure I was up for the task of treatment and told God so a few times.

When this happens to people, when we face an unexpected challenge — whether it's positive or negative — God's answer to our insecurities is usually a variation of six small but mighty words, "*But I will be with you!*" This He told Moses three times (in **Exodus 3:12, 4:12,** and **4:15**). And this He told me as well because that is the exact passage that I had planned to teach at a women's retreat just three days after receiving my news.

* * *

Let me tell you a little about myself so this book will make more sense. I have been married to my high school love for almost 47 years. We surrendered our lives to Jesus in our early 20s and have been in fulltime ministry for 42 of those years. For the last 34 years we have pastored a church in Ontario, Oregon which we started in December 1990. Somehow the Lord has seen fit to grow our local church body as well as our online ministry to the point where I no longer enjoy the luxury of anonymity.

When I realized the battle I would be facing and headed out that weekend to teach at a retreat, my husband took the opportunity to break the news to our church body and our online audience. Neither of us wears our emotions on our sleeves and both of us prefer to tuck all health-related information down deep, so as to not be noticed by anyone. But this would be different. A girl can hardly go through chemotherapy and act as if nothing has happened.

So, that Sunday morning in April, while I was gone, Paul shared about my situation from the pulpit after his regular teaching. He closed with a personal request that I not be inundated with questions and remedies; and he promised that I would find a way to keep everyone updated on my treatments and progress.

I agreed that it would be good to keep our church family, and my friends updated so they would know how to pray for me and know how I was doing, even though sharing that type of information didn't come naturally to me. Thus, I started a weekly blog. My first post was April 24, 2024 and my final post, 35 weeks later, was December 18, 2024.

During those weeks, while I was in treatment of one type or another, I wrote 35 devotions that were intended to encourage others to *Lean into the Presence of the Lord*. Those original blog posts are what you will find in this book — *35 Devotions for Challenging Times*. I've edited them slightly since I usually included a final paragraph with a health update that is irrelevant now. But, for the most part, these are the thoughts that the Lord gave me during those weeks with all the seasonal references intact as you journey with me from April through December.

I've written and taught dozens of women's Bible studies and over a hundred retreat sessions, but I've never received the consistent feedback from so many people as they encouraged me to put these devotions into book form.

We all have people in our lives who are natural encouragers, and I've learned to just let them *encourage away* without taking too much stock in what they say. But when other voices, who don't normally encourage, began to pop up with the same suggestion to compile these into book form, I wondered if I should take it to heart. And that is what I have done.

This is *not* a book about cancer, although I hope I've left just enough crumbs from my own challenges to be relatable and maybe even authentic. It's a book of devotions for any challenging season you might be facing. At the end of the day, isn't that most of us most of the time?

***

There is one sweet aspect to this journey that I didn't write into any of the devotions that I think you would enjoy, so I'll share that here.

The day after my diagnosis, while I was still processing all that needed to be done on the medical front, I was also weighing the wisdom of heading out of town to fulfill the retreat teaching commitment I had made. Being a bit of an analytical person by nature, I pulled out my journal, drew a vertical line and wrote *pros* and *cons* on the top of the two columns.

On the *pro* side of going through with the retreat I listed three main points:

- The church I was to teach for wouldn't have to make a last-minute scramble for a retreat speaker two days before their retreat. (A *pro* for them mostly.)

- Since the retreat was in the redwood forests of central California, I would be in a beautiful place to spend some time with the Lord and process the next chapter of my life. Nature is my jam when I need to hear from God, and this would be a *pro* for me.

- I might actually receive a blessing for having gone to teach, and I might make dozens of new friends that would be praying for me. (This actually happened.)

On the *con* side I could only think of one thing:

- I might not sleep well. But, I reasoned, that's been known to happen at home too — so it might not really count!

Although my analysis was complete, something was still lacking. I *needed* to actually hear from God. So, I sat with my Bible, like I've often done over the course of my life when big decisions are looming, and I asked God to speak to me through His Word. I asked for a specific Bible reference as I've done many times over the years and in the quiet of my waiting, I felt impressed that the Lord put into my heart **Isaiah 54:10**, which begins —

> *For the mountains may depart and the hills be removed, but my steadfast love shall not depart from you...*

I would have to say that the first half of the verse isn't exactly the most comforting word a woman with breast cancer could receive — and yet, it *was* strangely comforting. It was as if God was saying, "*if the worst case happens, I will still be with you.*"

But it was the second phrase that started a cascade of comfort and closeness that carried me through the summer. You see, I decided to put my normal Bible-reading plan on hold and begin a slow simmer in the Psalms during my treatment season. Since the Lord had given me this beautiful promise about His *steadfast love*, I decided to note every reference to *steadfast love* that I came across in my Psalm reading. Not only did I underline the phrase, but I noted "SL" (for Steadfast Love) in the margin of my Bible each time I came to it.

It didn't take me too long to observe all of the "SL" notations in my Bible and it didn't take me too long to realize that my Bible was becoming filled with *my initials*. The first week of my journey God told me, "*I will be with you*" because of the message I had prepared for that retreat. Then all along the way He organized this precious personalization in my Bible. How could I not face the days to come with courage? How could I not *lean into the presence of the Lord*?

My hope is that there will be something in one of these devotions that speaks to you as well, something that makes sense for your life, something that makes you realize that God sees your situation and "*He will be with you.*"

My love and blessings to you all as you read!

Sue

Leaning into the Lord

"God sometimes raises difficulties in the way of His people, that He may have the glory of subduing them, and helping His people over them." ~ Matthew Henry

As I've been processing this new season of my life that includes breast cancer treatment, I'm keenly aware that I'm entering into a completely different orbit of knowing the steadfast love of the Lord more personally and more deeply!

Since treatment hasn't technically begun yet, I simply want to share where I find myself and how God is comforting me, even as I walk through the doorway to treatment, surgery, and all that goes with a disease like this.

Last week, as the Lord planned it, I received my diagnosis only three days before I was to teach at a Women's Retreat in California. The pre-arranged text was the Exodus of the people of Israel out of Egypt. As they fled Egypt, they found themselves in an unexpected and troubling situation — God led them to a place where the Red Sea was before them and the Egyptian army came closing in behind. But God had a plan, not only for their rescue, but to declare His power and make sure everyone (including the Egyptians) knew **that He was the LORD (Exodus 14:4)**.

Even though the way in which He led His people was unexpected, they could always expect God's presence to be with them. In fact, that was the real theme of the retreat — **leaning into the presence of the Lord.** God had trained Moses ahead of time for this exact moment by telling him **"I will be with you" (Exodus 3:12)** and reminding him of that two more times.

Don't you find it interesting, as I do, that multiple times in my retreat message I reinforced this statement:

> *You can live with courage and overcome any emotion if you learn to lean into the presence of the Lord!*

Yep. I think that was part of the arrangement — God allowed me to go preach to myself and He let a room full of women listen in. (God tends to be very efficient that way)

And so, this is my resting place now for the next several months, *leaning into the presence of the Lord!* I'm probably a bit more private than the average gal. I dislike anything sensational. I don't care for much attention — especially health-related attention. But I'm realizing that a clear view of the Red Sea (looming difficulty) in people's lives can bring more glory to God than a dim view or no view at all. Therefore, I will agree to allow you a glimpse of the Red Sea that I'm facing so that you can be encouraged with the work of the Lord in the life of a simple follower of Jesus.

Here is my current condition. I have a fairly aggressive breast cancer that has extended into the lymph nodes. I've already met with my oncologist and tomorrow I will meet with my highly-recommended surgeon. Early next week my port will be installed and I'll be ready to begin chemotherapy. It's too soon to know the length of treatment or the timing of surgery, but I'm confident that everything will unfold in good order.

My love and blessings to all who care to read this—and my sincere thanks to all who have joined us in prayer,

Sue

A Summer Sabbatical

"Behold, the eye of the Lord is on those who fear him, on those who hope in his steadfast love."
Psalm 33:18

Today, May 1st, is what we used to call *May Day* when I was young — maybe people still use that term. In Minnesota it seemed to me like a holiday invented to put snow in the rear-view mirror and assure ourselves that summer was indeed on the way. All these years later, May signals a new season for me in a different, but good way.

I've begun to realize that God is ushering me into a *summer sabbatical!* Many people take sabbaticals — often they are carefully planned events. The point is usually a time of rest or travel or a dedicated time for continuing education or writing a book or something that a person has been yearning to do. Obviously, my summer sabbatical will be nothing like that, but I've come to realize that if a person has to do chemo, there is no better time to begin than May in order to enjoy everything that summer offers: sunshine, flowers, predictable weather, fewer germs, opportunities to be with people in outdoor settings...the list goes on and on. So, I'm super thankful to begin a treatment like this *now*.

In my last post, I used the word *aggressive* to describe the type of cancer that has become my enemy. *Aggressive* isn't all bad and in my case it may prove beneficial. All of those little cells with open and hungry mouths are about to gobble up a big surprise intended to make them shrink back in horror (okay that's a bit dramatic) but the point is, we have every hope that chemotherapy will prove quite effective on this cancer.

I also have another huge piece to be grateful for this week — all my labs, scans, and echos show **no cancer** lurking in other organs or bones! WOW! That news was huge for me! I know that God will walk with me through *any* of the cancer problems that could possibly arise but hearing the news that I merely have breast cancer now seems pretty doable and a huge reason for praise!

Maybe you are experiencing an un-planned sabbatical. In your planned sabbatical you would have been traveling or recreating or learning something new, but in this unexpected sabbatical you have no idea what you'll be doing — you only know that things will be different. Well, hop on board with me and we'll figure this out together.

Remember the first phrase of **Psalm 33:18** at the opening of this chapter, *"Behold, the eye of the Lord is on those who fear Him!"* Nothing in your life has taken God by surprise, His eye is firmly fixed on you.

Saturated in the Word

"The most valuable thing the Psalms do for me is to express the same delight in God which made David dance." ~ C. S. Lewis

Since my early twenties I've been an avid Bible reader. In fact, my hospital reading after giving birth to my firstborn was the book of Acts, which is probably not typical postpartum fare. Yet up until the age of 45 I had still never read through the entire Bible in one year's time.

That year I purchased a vintage hard-cover biography of Harry Ironside as a Christmas gift for one of my sons who was returning from Bible college. Ironside was a Bible expositor/pastor who served at Moody Bible Church in Chicago from 1930-1948. I'm never one to gift a book without reading it, so that December, it came to be that Ironside's biography made a big impression on me. I was inspired to read through the Bible that year and every year for the second half of my lifetime. Ironside had begun his annual read at age 13 and also made up for the first 13 years in arrears before he turned twenty.

In my retreats, I often encourage women that "*a woman of faith must saturate herself in the Word of God.*" That carries a whole different meaning than simply telling someone '*you should read your Bible.*' In fact, I've often quoted something that Elisabeth Elliott's father (Phillip Howard) wrote in one of the Christian periodicals he published:

> *"A Christian who is saturated with the Word is likely to have a calm, wholesome outlook on life; to be kept steady in the path of God's will in either joy or sorrow, wealth or poverty; he is likely to be a pleasant companion, not voluble in aimless talk; and he will not be overly disturbed by world conditions."* (Elisabeth Elliott, The Shaping of a Christian Family, 1992, p.5 6)

That sentence sums up the benefits of Bible consumption fairly well. I still have a few books of the Bible to finish for this year's pass to be complete, but currently, as part of my *Summer Sabbatical,* the Lord has sent me back to the Psalms for a do-over, as if I had missed something important.

I've appreciated the Psalms as much as the next person, but having a *real* enemy to fight has given the poetry of David (and others) added texture! I mean, I've personalized a Psalm here and there in my life. The Lord has lifted a handful of verses off the page to bring insight into life's situations. But, suddenly every single Psalm is highly personalized and carries great meaning, comfort, and encouragement.

For example, this from **Psalm 31:14-16** —

> *"But I trust in you, O Lord; I say, "You are my God." My times are in your hand; rescue me from the hand of my enemies and from my persecutors! Make your face shine on your servant; save me in your steadfast love!*

Maybe I've never had a *real* enemy before — an enemy that was bent on destroying me, but suddenly I completely understand David's *real* enemies in the Psalms and I don't have one bit of a problem asking God to be victorious over my enemy, to in fact, destroy my enemy.

How about this from **Psalm 40:10** —

> *"I have not hidden your deliverance within my heart; I have spoken of your faithfulness and your salvation; I have not concealed your steadfast love and your faithfulness from the great congregation."*

That resonates with me because I believe in the power of God, and I also believe in the efficacy of treatments. But at the end of the day, God is always the one who delivers, and that reality I do not want to conceal. I want to make his love and faithfulness known in the *great congregation.*

So, this brings me to share about my treatments. In the words of my surgeon, *I have jumped on the chemo train and will be riding it until mid-September.* That is the point of chemotherapy — get started and keep going.

If you are praying for me, I have two requests for this summer, no three:

1) That my health would stay strong so as to avoid any breaks in treatment that would prolong this phase.

2) That the Lord would enable these chemicals to attack my enemy.

3) That I would embrace a season of rest.

Unexpected Paths

> *"The Israelites were dressed for fighting when they left the land of Egypt."* Exodus 13:18 (EXB)

I'm amazed that I've gotten this far in life with only one significant memory of being completely under-dressed! Paul and I lived in the Seattle area in the mid-eighties and somehow, we missed the memo that a particular church function was a dress-up event. *Who plans those anyway?* We arrived in our normal casual clothes with our normal casual toddlers on our normal hips and immediately felt our deficiency keenly.

We all know there are some clothes for gardening and other clothes for weddings. We dress differently to eat popcorn and watch a movie than to go to the ballet. In general, people dress according to their expectations — taking into consideration the next event on their schedule. The nation of Israel was no different. In the post-Passover morning light, God's people began a miraculous exodus out of Egypt toward the land God promised them and they were dressed according to their expectations of what that path would be like.

Look how **Exodus 13:17-18** describes that journey:

> *When Pharaoh sent the people out of Egypt, God did not lead them on the road through the Philistine country, though that was the shortest way. God said, "If they have to fight, they might change their minds and go back to Egypt." So God led them through the desert toward the Red Sea. The Israelites were <u>dressed for fighting</u> when they left the land of Egypt.*

Hmm, they were *dressed for fighting* (EXB), *equipped for battle* (ESV) even though that clearly wasn't the way God was leading them. They thought the next event on their schedule was to leave Egypt via the *Way of the Philistines*, which would have required battle and battle attire — but they were mistaken.

I'm sure you've had expectations in life and just like me you emotionally *dressed for them*. You may have thought the next event on your schedule was marriage, or children, a particular job, retirement, or a certain type of ministry. But then you realized *God did not lead you on that road.* In Israel's case, God had a far better path in mind for His kids. Granted, it looked scarier in the moment, but it got them to their destination with no casualties and with the bonus of God's power fully on display.

The same is often true in our lives. God has a good path in mind for us and occasionally it may look scarier than our expected path.

Look how **Psalm 25: 9-10** describes God's paths:

> *"He leads the humble in what is right, and teaches the humble his way. All the paths of the LORD are steadfast love and faithfulness, for those who keep his covenant and his testimonies."*

The path that God leads us on is His responsibility, but how we respond to that path is our responsibility. Paul and I had no ability to turn that 80's dress-up event into a casual affair just to suit our expectations and our dress. In our lives we'll only make ourselves miserable if we insist that our path matches our expectations, rather than humbly changing our expectations to match God's path. We would be happier and healthier if we would learn the art of quickly noting how God is leading, embracing the path of His choosing, and changing up our emotional and spiritual attire to match His path.

You've probably guessed how this topic relates to me. I've had to quickly change my emotional attire this summer since I entered this season *dressed for ministry.* My expectation was traveling and teaching at several retreats — but God chose quite a different path — He has chosen for me to be riding the *Chemo Train* (hereafter referred to merely as *The Train*). It's all good — *all the paths of the Lord are steadfast love and faithfulness.*

How does this topic relate to you? Has God allowed you to travel on a different path than you expected? Are you making swift adjustments to the reality of how God is leading you, or holding on to your previous expectations? I hope you're choosing the *happy and healthy* route by embracing God's plan.

Secret Clubs

"...so that we can comfort those in any trouble with the comfort we ourselves have received from God." **2 Corinthians 1:4 (NIV84)**

Sitting on a little patch of squashed-down weeds, under an elm grove, behind my mother's vegetable garden, my older sister and I met weekly for our *Secret Club*. We called it the *Good Deed Doers Club* — I know, go ahead and roll your eyes. We were about six and eleven and from what I can remember our club meetings consisted of writing a list of helpful things we could do and a collection of the weekly ten cent dues. I have no memory of following through on our deeds, nor do I recall the funds ever being put to use, so perhaps I should yet call for an audit of that club account which was held suspiciously in the hands of the eleven-year-old. *

Those are the types of *Secret Clubs* children create while waiting for life to usher them into other *Clubs*. Eventually we all enter into unique clubs of one type or another — some by choice, others by force. Some are a delight, some are formed from trials, some are public and some are more secret.

I've been in the *Pastor's Wives Club* for over 42 years and still belong. I was in the *Homeschool Moms Club* for 26 years — I think that should have earned me a trip to Hawaii as a reward. I'm threatening to be a legitimate member of the *Sourdough Makers Club*. But now, I've suddenly become acquainted with a new *Secret Club* that I really didn't have much reason to pay any attention to before this year — it's the *Breast Cancer Club (BC Club,* or just *C Club)*.

Suddenly women from the *BC Club* approach me out of the blue and we form an immediate connection. They have something to say, something to share, and a special way of encouraging me. Just this week a woman whom I had never met (but we have a recent mutual acquaintance) travelled sixty miles to chat with me for an hour during my infusion and bring me a bag of extremely thoughtful and useful products. Why? She's in *The Club*. The *Club* creates a natural sense of belonging. But there is one more aspect beyond just belonging — God put an inner drive in us to comfort others with the comfort we ourselves have received.

Here's how the Apostle Paul put it in **2 Corinthians 1:3-4 (NIV84)** —

> *"Praise be to the God and Father of our Lord Jesus Christ, the Father of compassion and the God of all comfort, who comforts us in all our troubles, so that we can comfort those in any trouble with the comfort we ourselves have received from God."*

I think it's baked into our soul to be useful to others. When we have received comfort from God in a particular area of life we are compelled to turn around and invest in others.

You've probably passed through many *Clubs* in your lifetime — some *secret*, some *not-so-secret*. You may have been in the *Singles Club* for a season, the *Unemployed Club*, the *Newlywed Club*, the *Launching a Business Club*. Some of those clubs last only for a season.

But there are other clubs that last a lifetime or at least affect us for a lifetime — having a *Special Needs Child, Losing a Child, Widowhood* (even if you remarry). There is a secret club for *Parents of Prodigals* and an even more special club for parents of substance-abuse prodigals. There is a tender club for those who have been abused/abandoned by the ones who promised to love them. If you have found yourself in one of these *secret clubs,* your first instinct was probably to look for the door and get out of the club. That's not always possible. But what is possible is to *find the comfort of the Father of compassion, who comforts us in all our troubles.* Once we tap into God's comfort in our *Secret Club* we are not only comforted ourselves, but we are able to partner with the Lord in bringing comfort to other members of *The Club.* And they need our comfort — especially when they first walk through the door of the club!

My encouragement is *don't waste your pain* — make the best use of whatever Club you find yourself a member of by comforting others in that Club.

Note* After the publication of this devotion, my sisters helped me walk back in time and I wanted to report that a few *good deeds* were actually accomplished AND the club dues were put to good use to buy Easter egg candy for the family! Audit Complete!

Under Construction

"The road to success is usually under construction" ~ Arnold Palmer

It's graduation season and tonight Paul and I will be attending our grand-daughter's ceremony after having enjoyed her party over the weekend. (Parenthetically, I LOVE being the grand parent and merely showing up with only a few small, assigned tasks — this is an awesome season of life!)

During graduation season, I would say the word most popularly used would be *congratulations* — and the second would be *success*. We say things like, *'we wish you every success in whatever path you choose'*. That's a very kind thing to say to graduates, however, it might be more helpful to quote the late professional golfer Arnold

Palmer, *'just know that the road to success is usually under-construction!'* That sentiment would get it right out there to plan for a bumpy ride ahead!

The mere mention of Arnold Palmer takes me back to the Sunday afternoons of my childhood. My mom and dad took a day of rest seriously, so after church and a fantastic dinner prepared by my mother, they were *off duty*. They usually napped, but I seem to remember a lot of golf on TV — which I thought was the most boring activity anyone could possibly think up.

Arnold Palmer was exactly my parents' age, and he was just about single-handedly responsible for elevating the appreciation of golf from an elite and entitled audience to a sport for the average American. That was my dad, an average American and somehow he could relate to Arnold because his road, like my dad's, was *usually under-construction*.

Reflecting on his career, Palmer wrote, *"Perhaps the reason people enjoyed watching me play so much was that they could relate to my predicaments. I was often where they were as I came down the stretch—in the rough, in the trees, or up the creek."*

Isn't that the truth in life? There is no straight, level, sunny path from the beginning of our journey to the end. In spiritual terms, we might want to change the wording from *'road to success'* to *'finishing well'*. As Christians, our goal isn't so much to be *successful* in life as it is to do what God has assigned us and *finish well*. We often say we want to hear those words, **"Well done, good and faithful servant" (Matthew 25:21)**. It seems to me that the road to *finishing well* is also usually under construction.

I love reading biographies and I have read hundreds of them. One common denominator with all the men and women whose lives I've admired is that they often found themselves *in the rough, in the trees, or up the creek* at multiple points. I cannot name one admired person, past or present, whose game of life seemed to drive happily straight down the fairway. And that doesn't happen for us either!

We probably all hope for the fairway of life, but that's not our experience. Sometimes, even our most prayed-over decisions can land us in the *rough*; our long-awaited opportunities can seem to *bounce off the trees*; and some unexpected life events leave us with the sound of *ker-plunk* and the sight of *ripples* from the waterway.

So, what is one to do? What is the advice to the graduate? What is the advice for our own life? Here are a few morsels from the Bible that might speak to the task of persevering through *road construction* in life:

#1 Hitting construction in life is an experience that is common to all:

> *"Count it all joy, my brothers, <u>when</u> you meet trials of various kinds, for you know that the testing of your faith produces steadfastness. And let steadfastness have its full effect, that you may be perfect and complete, lacking in nothing."* **James 1:2-4**

#2 Focus on the Lord's work in your life rather than on your personal skills:

> *"And I am sure of this, that he who began a good work in you will bring it to completion at the day of Jesus Christ."* **Philippians 1:6**

#3 Regardless of what comes your way, put your head down and keep moving forward:

> *"Therefore, my beloved brothers, be steadfast, immovable, always abounding in the work of the Lord, knowing that in the Lord your labor is not in vain."* **1 Corinthians 15:58**

If *you personally* happen to be *in the rough, in the trees, or up the creek*, can I encourage you with those Scriptures above? Maybe there is someone in your life that you need to encourage as well! One thing we have in common as Christians is that we're all endeavoring to *finish well.* I would hope that we can help each other do just that.

Burger Season

"But to Hannah he gave a double portion, because he loved her" 1 Samuel 1:5

The summer months have arrived and we're all about to consume more backyard burgers than we bargained for! It makes perfect sense because burgers are a staple of American social life and summer life.

I have opinions about burgers as I'm sure you do. On our recent *local vacation* Paul and I finally made it to the California-turned-Idaho IN-N-OUT Burgers in Meridian. Our family tribe grabbed our boxes of burgers and walked over to enjoy them outdoors seated near the fountain in **The Village** shopping center.

Now, IN-N-OUT has its place: nostalgia for some, budget friendly for others, and still others wouldn't dream of going solo — it's a social experience. It might not be your fav, but I would guess that you do have a favorite hamburger place, whether it's a chain or a little drive-in — and if you *really* want a burger to savor — you know where you want to go!

My favorite burger on our end of the valley is actually at our local Japanese restaurant, Ogawas. Don't get me wrong, I love me some rice bowls too, but I think their burgers are perfection. They are cooked smash-burger style with crispy edges that extend beyond the border of the not-too-lofty bun (which eliminates the side-of-mouth ache in trying to open too wide). And the accompanying fries are pretty good too. It's a strange favorite burger place, but its mine.

When our kids were little, the economic choices for our family were pretty much Wendy's and Burger King. I mean, we weren't wealthy, but we didn't have to resort to McDonalds.

Years later when our kids were still home, but grown, we hosted a young adults group called 18-28 in our home on Sunday nights. Paul considered it his favorite teaching time of the week. Coincidentally, McDonalds happened to be offering $.39 Sunday Cheeseburgers during that era, so after the Bible study dozens of young adults would toss all available loose change into a pile on the floor (along with anything found in my couch cushions). One or two guys would head over to McDs to pick up as many cheeseburgers as the cash pile could procure.

On occasion, there would be an extra and someone would extend it in front of me with an 18yo smile and say, *"Here Mrs. L, we brought you a cheeseburger"*. What is one to do in that situation except smile back and say, *'thank you'*?

There is a woman in the Bible that had her heart set on something important and basically had a couple of *cheeseburgers* extended to her. Well, it wasn't *exactly* that way, but the beginning of 1 Samuel introduces us to Hannah, who had one craving in life, she desired to have a child. Her husband loved her, he knew her lack, he understood that she was barren, but the best he could come up with to encourage her was to offer her more *cheeseburgers* than he gave to the others.

Actually, here's what the text tells us in **1 Samuel 1:4-5** —

> *"On the day when Elkanah sacrificed, he would give portions to Peninnah his wife and to all her sons and daughters. But to Hannah he gave a double portion, because he loved her, though the Lord had closed her womb."*

There was no possible way that Elkanah could have fixed Hannah's problem — only God could meet her need. The best he could do was to offer love and support in his own way, albeit somewhat awkward.

When we have an ache in our hearts because something important is lacking in our life, or we are grieving a significant loss, people's gestures of love and affirmation can fall short, but the point is they *are* gestures of love and affirmation, and they do have significant meaning and even healing properties!

We'll take a deeper look at Hannah's life next week, but for this short devotion, our main point is *don't expect people around you to be God — they are not — they cannot fix what is wrong!* Most of them are doing the best they can by offering love and support in whatever way they are able and sometimes we just need to soak in all of those acts of love a bit more.

Proverbs 27:9 (NLV) says —

> *"Oil and perfume make the heart glad, so are a man's words sweet to his friend."*

Whether you need to be the giver of a double portion right now, or maybe you need to graciously receive the double portion — there is probably a message for all of us in Elkanah's actions.

I have truly received a mountain of encouragement from all who have said, and done, and sent, and offered, and prayed support in my direction. Every single gesture is meaningful and healing, even if it doesn't fix my core problem.

So, if a friend shows up at your door this week with *two cheeseburgers* — just smile, thank them, feel the awkward love and invite them in — but if you see yellow arches on the wrapper, *you don't have to eat them!*

No Longer Sad

"Hannah went her way and ate, and her face was no longer sad." 1 Samuel 1:18

Many people know the Biblical figure **Hannah** from the Old Testament. She was the mother of Samuel, the child given to the service of the Lord, who later became a central figure in the days of David. There must be something about her life that resonates with people (women in particular) because, of all the Bible lessons I've taught, the narrative of Hannah is THE most popular by quite a bit.

Perhaps Hannah personifies our human condition.

- She faced a certain brand of personal difficulty — not being able to conceive a child. We all face some type of personal difficulties in life as well.

- She suffered from annoying interactions with those close to her — her husband meant well but his efforts to cheer her missed the mark — her rival purposefully provoked her — the spiritual figure in her world misunderstood her and accused her of being drunk. We also have challenging people in our lives that can cause similar irritations.

All of the situations in Hannah's life created a recipe for a nasty brew of emotions and, you guessed it, sometimes we also experience a nasty brew of emotions. But the beauty of her story lies in the choices she made as to what to do with her emotions.

Look how intense Hannah's emotions were as she went to the Lord (**1 Samuel 1:10-11**) *Hannah was <u>deeply distressed</u> and prayed to the LORD and <u>wept bitterly</u>.* This was a woman carrying *hard emotions* and the reality is that we sometimes find our path filled with *hard emotions*.

We can't always control *how we feel*, but we can control what we *do* about *how we feel*. Hannah gives us a simple, yet profound example of what to do with *hard emotions*, the ONLY answer is to run to the Lord and *pour out your soul* (**v.15**). It's okay to be in *deep distress and to weep bitterly* (**v.10**), to have *great anxiety* and *vexation* (**v.16**), those are real emotions, they're *hard emotions*. But it's not okay to be inconsolable and unable to receive refreshment from the Lord.

In Hannah's case, the very person who accused her of being a babbling drunk gave her a promise of the exact refreshment she was seeking! (**v.17**) *Eli answered, "Go in peace, and the God of Israel grant your petition that you have made to him."* How easy it would have been for emotions to rule the day and for her to lash out something to the effect that *Eli understood nothing of what was going on in her life* and *how dare he even say anything to her*!

But Hannah instinctively knew something about the Lord that later Psalmists would write in many different ways — when a person cries out to the Lord, He hears!

> **Psalm 34:6** *In my desperation I prayed, and the LORD listened; he saved me from all my troubles.*

Hannah was *looking* for refreshment and willing to receive refreshment. I love how the episode at the temple is quickly wrapped up in **v.18 "*Then the woman went her way and ate, and her face was no longer sad.*"** Isn't that a simple goal in life? To be no longer *sad*? The brief number of verses might threaten to over-simplify the matter, yet sometimes we naturally over-complicate the matter, so I'm okay with it.

Maybe there is a nugget here for someone reading today. You might have small but *hard emotions*, or large and *hard emotions.* Maybe peeking into Hannah's life is just the inspiration you need to take your *hard emotions* to the Lord. Or maybe someone reading today needs a new Bible study and 1 Samuel might be just the thing!

You can follow the QR code to download the study guide (or order a paper copy) and get started and see how the Lord might minister to you.

Ebenezer

"Here I raise my Ebenezer, hither by Thy help I've come." ~ Robert Robinson

Have you ever played a word-association game where someone says a particular word and then you say the first thing that comes to mind? For example, if I say *salt*, you might respond with *pepper*; or if I say *beach* you might say *tropical* or *Waikiki*. What if I said *Ebenezer*? Many people might say *Scrooge* — but a few people with a well-worn hymnal might come back with *'here I raise my...'* quoting from the familiar line in the hymn *Come Thou Fount of Every Blessing* (noted above).

It's a great hymn with a great back story (that we'll save for a different time). If this hymn was part of your childhood, you probably sang about your *Ebenezer* long before you ever understood what an *Ebenezer* was. If you still don't know, you're about to learn!

Remember that baby of Hannah's? Samuel? Well, he grew up to be both a prophet and judge over the nation of Israel. During one particular battle with Israel's nemesis neighbors, the Philistines, Samuel was able to unite the people to seek the Lord's help and God responded in a mighty way:

> *But the LORD thundered with a mighty sound that day against the Philistines and threw them into confusion, and they were defeated before Israel. And the men of Israel went out from Mizpah and pursued the Philistines and struck them...* **1 Samuel 7:10-11**

That was awesome...a reason to rejoice for sure, but Samuel wanted to make sure they didn't quickly forget about the Lord's intervention, so:

> *Samuel took a stone and set it up between Mizpah and Shen and called its name Ebenezer; for he said, "Till now the LORD has helped us."* **1 Samuel 7:12**

That is the essence of an *Ebenezer* — marking the Lord's help in our lives. I actually like the NIV rendering, *"Thus far the Lord has helped us."*

During retreats, I often encourage the ladies to reflect on what God has done in their lives. Our natural path is one of forgetfulness, so we need to be purposeful in recounting and celebrating God's work. I think one of the best ways, one of the most natural ways, is to make use of regularly occurring significant events in our lives as an opportunity to *raise an Ebenezer*. For example, on your birthday — take time to commemorate the specific work of God in your life in the previous year — *raise some Ebenezers*. New Year's Day might be another good opportunity, or the beginning or ending of a school year; whatever is significant in your rhythm of life.

The beauty of *raising an Ebenezer* is obvious.

- The more we celebrate God's help in the past, the more encouraged we will be to ask for His help in the future.

- The more we remind ourselves of God's help and faithfulness, the easier it becomes to share those stories with our children and grandchildren. They need to hear stories of God's faithfulness to build their own faith.

If you haven't raised an *Ebenezer* recently (or ever) today would be a good time to do just that! I have personally come to a significant moment to *raise an Ebenezer* — and that is the completion of phase one of my chemo treatment — *thus far has the Lord helped me!* Praise the Lord that phase is in the rearview mirror.

Now I am encouraged to ask for His help for phase two, which will begin this coming Tuesday and run for twelve weeks. My prayer requests are the same: 1) that the chemo would be effective, 2) that I would stay healthy enough to stay on schedule, and 3) that I would embrace this season of rest, this *summer sabbatical*.

When Life Leaves You Flattened

"The LORD preserves the simple; when I was brought low, he saved me." Psalm 116:6

The previous devotion was all about raising an Ebenezer, meaning to recognize what God has accomplished in our lives in order to build up our faith for the future. For my part, I was thanking the Lord for helping me through phase one of my treatment. I was sincere when I wrote it last week and I'm still thankful, even though the day after those thoughts were published, I experienced my hardest day yet.

In cancer treatment, it can be difficult to predict exactly when a few too many side-effects will collide to create a perfect storm. And the same is true for life in general — it can be difficult to predict when a few too many challenges will collide to flatten us to about 15% of ourselves. And that's where I was last Thursday — about 15% of myself.

Before we go on, I want to say a few things: 1) I'm back up to about 90% as I write this, 2) My oncologist told me yesterday that the first phase of chemo I took was probably *the most* difficult of all therapies across the entire cancer spectrum — glad he didn't tell me that up front, 3) I never wanted to drag you through the grit of treatment but sometimes that could make it appear as though it's *no big deal*, when it really is a *big deal*, 4) I tend to turn everything into a learning experience and that's why I titled these thoughts, "*When Life Leaves You Flattened.*"

As I've been *simmering in the Psalms* this summer, one thing I've grown to re-appreciate about the Psalmists is their ability to both lay out the gritty truth of their situation and apply their trust in the Lord over the top of the grit. Here's a good example that happened to be in my reading line-up last Thursday:

> *I cry to you, O Lord; I say, "You are my refuge, my portion in the land of the living." Attend to my cry, for I am brought very low! Deliver me from my persecutors, for they are too strong*

for me! Bring me out of prison, that I may give thanks to your name! **(Psalm 142:5-7)**

If you lay that petition over the top of **your** current troubles in life, it might seem a bit over-dramatic at first; but I think we should resist that notion. When we are the ones suffering — it *is* dramatic, we *are* brought very low, we *do* need God's deliverance, so that we *can* give thanks another day.

Here are two thoughts in the midst of suffering through a current battle that has brought you low:

God never grows tired of us asking. He actually delights when we ask for deliverance, or help, or healing, or sustaining, or whatever word seems to fit. On my bad day, my eyes wouldn't cooperate to either read a book or look at a screen and my body wouldn't cooperate to move, so I sat in the recliner and prayed more that day than the whole previous week combined. A lot of my prayers were for me (like the psalmist), but I prayed for others as well — because we tend to recognize or remember the suffering of others when we are brought low.

Consider exactly who your enemy is and isn't. My suffering was largely due to chemo drugs — but chemo is not my enemy — chemo is actually an ally in this battle, but in the moment everything I was suffering was a direct result of its presence in my life. Isn't that the truth in our regular life battles? Your spouse is not your enemy, your teen is not your enemy, your toddler, your mother, your car repairs are not your enemy even though your suffering might be the direct result of their presence in your life. Still, they are not your enemy.

The temptation exists to delete painful things out of our lives, even if they are not our enemy, just to get some relief. But this option is misguided. There is a remedy for pain and suffering and it's the same remedy the Psalmists always employed — *cry out to the Lord for help*!

Again, I want to say that God was gracious to sustain me through a very low dip and I'm trusting He will do that in the future, should the need arise. I'm trusting He will also do it for *you* when you face pain or suffering, particularly from something or someone who isn't your real enemy.

It Won't Always be this Way

"Nothing paralyzes our lives like the attitude that things can never change." ~ Warren Wiersbe

I am naturally an optimistic person. I think my optimism bugs some people, but one of my favorite phrases is, *'it won't always be this way'*. That's actually a great phrase of comfort for a lot of things in life — my own experience included. I have endured several uncomfortable elements in the process of cancer treatment — but I can always say to myself, *it won't always be this way*, I won't be on chemo forever.

However, some things happen in our lives that actually *will* always *be this way,* some people *are* on chemo for life; some have lost a loved one and that hole will always exist; some have a severely special needs child who will always rely on them; some have faced a life-long debilitation from an accident. I actually have many friends moving forward in the midst of a difficult or painful situation that will remain for life and never really resolve to that hoped-for memory in the rearview mirror.

Those difficult situations require a bit more than a velvety phrase of optimistic encouragement. They actually require something we call *patient perseverance*! UGH! *Perseverance* is so much work. One definition of *perseverance* I had written in my journal years ago was, *'the grit required to continue to press forward, despite opposition.'* That pretty much sums it up...but where in the world do we drum up the *grit*?

Well, you won't be surprised at my answer — we need to ask the Lord for the *grit*, I mean, the kind of patient *perseverance* required to not only move forward but serve the Lord and honor Him in the situations we find ourselves.

I have a couple thoughts I'd like to share, but first, let me share the entire quote from Warren Wiersbe, which I abbreviated above:

> *"Nothing paralyzes our lives like the attitude that things can never change. We need to re-*

> *mind ourselves that God can change things. Outlook determines outcome. If we see only the problems, we will be defeated; but if we see the possibilities in the problems, we can have victory."*

Even though our circumstances might not change externally, God can change our outlook internally — and that IS change — that IS God changing things.

What are some ways God changes our outlook on life? I've thought of three:

Our Soul: When the Psalms mentions *our soul*, it generally refers to our emotions and our thoughts — what we think about and what we feel. When we get that sinking feeling that things *will always be this way*, the lion's share of our battle is **mental**. The Psalms often remind us to intentionally point our soul to God, as in this Psalm from my reading line-up today:

> *To you, O LORD, I lift up my soul. O my God, in you I trust; let me not be put to shame; let not my enemies* exult over me.* **Psalm 25:1-2**
> (*Where the enemy is represented by some difficulty that will never go away in our life.)

Our Expectations: Note the excellent advice from Mr. Wiersbe: *"If we see only the problems, we will be defeated;*

but if we see the possibilities in the problems, we can have victory. The Apostle Paul said the same thing with a different vocabulary,

> *"But he said to me, "My grace is sufficient for you, for my power is made perfect in weakness." Therefore, I will boast all the more gladly of my weaknesses, so that the power of Christ may rest upon me. For the sake of Christ, then, I am content with weaknesses, insults, hardships, persecutions, and calamities. For when I am weak, then I am strong."* **(1 Corinthians 12:9-11)**

Our Tribe: God never intended us to walk through life solo, He fashioned The Body in such a way that we suffer together and rejoice together. By *tribe*, I obviously mean the part of the Body of Christ that you regularly hang with. Having a tribe that knows your difficulty and yet will encourage you with regard to your *soul* and your *expectations* means the world.

Look how Paul conveyed this (and how one sweet friend that I've never met encouraged me this week):

> *"If one member suffers, all suffer together; if one member is honored, all rejoice together."* **(1 Corinthians 12:26)**

Paul's words above end on a positive tone, but *The Preacher's* words in Ecclesiastes end with a sober warning on the same subject of finding and cultivating that *tribe* before the need arises:

> *"If either of them falls down, one can help the other up. But pity anyone who falls and has no one to help them up."* **(Ecclesiastes 4:10)**

The summary is that some of our suffering won't always be this way — and some of our suffering will remain. But that doesn't mean that God can't change our suffering into something useful, doable, profitable, if we remember to *lift up our soul, submit our expectations* and *find our tribe*!

Perplexing Decisions

"The LORD will guide you always; he will satisfy your needs in a sun-scorched land and will strengthen your frame. You will be like a well-watered garden, like a spring whose waters never fail." Isaiah 58:11 (NIV84)

I think we could effectively sort people into age groups with one simple question, *"how many varieties of cereal were on the grocery shelf when you were ten years old?"*

I didn't have a deprived childhood, but our cereal cupboard contained: Rice Krispies, Raisin Bran, and Wheaties, and I don't recall getting in on any purchasing decisions at the store. My own kids were occasionally granted cereal choosing privileges as if it were a genie wish. It's just too confusing and consuming to choose between hundreds of boxes of different grains, flavors, sugar content and fun-factor. Our own big box store here in town has floor to ceiling boxes and bags on both sides of an aisle that seems to extend indefinitely.

Cereal is on my mind, because, after not really buying or eating it for years, it seems to be the breakfast that sits with my palette lately. I'm hoping for a return to my normal peanut butter toast and coffee before the year is over, but for now I feel a bit like a *ten-year-old* again making my cereal choices and pouring my milk.

Maybe you're not in the *cereal world* these days like me, but maybe you have *real decisions* to make. Maybe you get overwhelmed with decisions in life. Maybe you find yourself confused and consumed with too many options or perplexed with too few options.

I was reminded recently of a verse that became very special to me over twenty years ago. I was soaking in the teaching at a Pastors Wives Retreat and our dear Kay Smith (wife of pastor Chuck Smith — both with the Lord) was teaching on **Isaiah 58:11**. I don't recall the weighty decisions I was facing (twenty years tends to make molehills out of those mountains), but I remember the Lord gently urging me to seek Him for guidance.

The first phrase of that verse says, **"The LORD will guide you always..."** but it was the second phrase that helped me to grip and personalize the first, **"...*he will satisfy your needs in a sun-scorched land...*"** That *was* and *is* my address in life, having been planted by the Lord in Ontario, Oregon. After all, it's projected to reach 109 degrees today and if that's not sun-scorched, I'm not sure what is. Our environmental need for water is obvious and ongoing, so the remainder of the verse brings yet more comfort, *"...you will be like a well-watered garden, like a spring whose waters never fail."* As a gardener, I know what it means to depend on irrigation, and as a Christian I also know what it means to depend on the Lord.

But, back to the first phrase — **The Lord will guide you always!** What a comfort to be able to rely on God to guide us in our perplexing decisions and to know that His guidance can be compared to a dependable and sustainable spring of water in a land where water doesn't come easy, or at all, in July.

So, what is your perplexity in life right now? I'm sure it's much more serious than cereal choices. We face important, sometimes crucial decisions every day: education options for our kids, job decisions, elder care for our parents, relational decisions, staying or leaving decisions. Then there are the critical *right-now* decisions at a time of crisis when the next five minutes will affect the next five years. Don't we want to have a verse like this in our mind? To know that **The Lord will guide us always.** It's just a matter of asking.

What prevents us from asking? We may feel we should be smart enough to navigate our own path. We may feel God is disinterested in our day-to-day life. We may feel our current distance from God and realize we're out of the habit of talking over such things. All of these erroneous thoughts can and should be captured and set right.

Now, just to be fair, the context of the entire chapter of **Isaiah 58** is centered around God's people walking in a sense of agreement with Him — representing His character in how they react and respond to the world and people around them. You might want to read the entire chapter. In fact, you also might also want to read **Psalm 36**, which I think dovetails beautifully. But the point of this short devotion is to remind you and me that God is waiting and willing to guide us in our tough decisions and that His guidance will feel to us like a life-giving spring of water in a hot, dry, barren spot in life.

I've had to make a few important decisions related to care-providers and treatment. I had no idea which way to go or even how to find the resources. As we say, '*they don't teach you this in school.*' So, it has blessed me so much when my husband has grabbed my hand, and we've simply prayed together for God's guidance. In the middle of a desert, He has been faithful to point us in the right direction and I know He will do the same for you in the middle of your sun-scorched land.

Don't Worry About Anything

"Therefore do not worry about tomorrow, for tomorrow will worry about itself. Each day has enough trouble of its own." Matthew 6:34 (NIV84)

I've been trying my hardest to finish a lengthy book that was begun a few years ago — <u>Martin Luther</u>, by Eric Metaxas. Actually, Paul and I started it together as a read-aloud during car trips, but 16th century German names and locations can get a little laborious to pronounce, so we set it aside. Well, this is my summer to check off the pile of books that have been set aside.

It's a great history book, and having now been to Germany, especially having walked the streets of Worms, I find the book all the more interesting. But even more fascinating to me than the story of the reformer's life is the story of his marriage to Katie, the former Katharina von Bora who was sent to a convent at age five. Eventually, Luther left his position as a monk and Katharina as a nun and Luther (42) and Katie (29) married and their lively relationship (including six children) began.

She was the quintessential homesteader and could have been a successful influencer in today's Instagram world where so many young women want chickens, a garden, herbal remedies, and fresh sourdough. Katharina herded, milked, and slaughtered cattle; made butter and cheese; brewed beer; fished from their pond, planted and harvested a garden and a fruit orchard; all while managing their 40-room home, which was an abandoned monastery called the Black Cloister. Luther affectionately called her *"The Morning Star of Wittenberg"*, or *"Kitty, my rib"*; she respectfully called him *"Doctor"*.

The point of this writing, however, is not their interesting marriage, but the fact that even intelligent, devoted, and accomplished Christians can fall into anxiety and worry. Luther himself was given to depression and hypochondria; Katie worried endlessly while *The Doctor* was traveling and away from her watchful eye. Maybe you also have your points of worry.

In our opening Scripture, Jesus exhorted his hearers, *"do NOT worry"*; **Psalm 37** begins with *"Fret NOT..."*; **Philippians 4:6** says, *"Do NOT be anxious about anything..."* Well, that solves everything, right? Now that we've been informed by those Scriptures we'll never worry again about a thing! Actually, it's not that easy, is it? We need constant reminders, maybe daily, and sometimes it doesn't hurt for someone to warn us about how futile (and damaging) our worry really is.

I learned from a different writing about Katharina Luther that once, while Luther was traveling, he sent the kind of reminder I'm referring to in a letter to his dear wife:

> *"To the saintly, worrying Lady Katherine Luther, doctor at Zulsdorf and Wittenberg, my gracious dear wife: We thank you heartily for being so worried that you can't sleep, for since you started worrying about us...and no doubt due to your worry, a big stone, save for the dear angels, would have fallen and crushed us like a mouse in a trap. If you don't stop worrying, I'm afraid the earth will swallow us."* (50 Women Every Christian Should Know, DeRusha, 2014, p. 55)

And Katie took her turn as well, even though she nursed Luther's many difficulties and infirmities, she knew when a simple pantomime would prove to be a sturdy reminder. One day, when Luther was depressed, Katie put on a black dress. Luther asked her: *"Are you going to a funeral?"* "No," she responded, *"but since you act as though God is dead, I wanted to join you in the mourning!"*

Are you worrying about something right now, as though God is dead? Do you go through your day as though He no longer sees or cares about the details of your life? Jesus' words in the Sermon on the Mount (**Matthew 6**, where our focus verse came from) reminds us that our Heavenly Father sees and knows what is going on in our life and what we need, and He will provide for us.

There *is* something we can do to replace worry, depression, hypochondria and it is most simply expressed in a children's song that all of my kids used to sing:

> *Don't worry about anything, but pray about everything, tell God your needs and don't forget to thank Him.*

Sometimes it also doesn't hurt to have someone close to us remind us how ridiculous worrying really is. I maybe wouldn't suggest going the black dress route unless you have a well-established relationship for that kind of loving sarcasm. But it might be your privilege this week to be the person who reminds others of the futility of worry and the necessity for prayer.

Stepping or Stopping?

"We can make our plans, but the LORD determines our steps." Proverbs 16:9 (NLT)

A phrase crossed my path this week that made a lot of sense to me — here is it: *"God watches over our steps and our stops"*. We may be familiar with some of the wonderful verses like the one above (**Proverbs 16:9**) about God guiding our *steps*. We love those verses! I'm particularly geared to the thought of forward progress. To *me, steps* equal progress. That's what we want in life, to move forward, to make progress, to cross things off our list, to feel accomplished, to get things done. We even monitor our steps on our smart watches and sometimes they even give us a visual and audio reward for completing our goals for the day.

But I think we sometimes make a leap of logic and believe that since we value forward progress so much, God must value it just as highly. Certainly, He must also be cheering our forward movement toward getting things done and that factors into how He *determines our steps*.

You can see why I had to contemplate that phrase "*God watches over our steps and our stops.*" Maybe, just maybe, God determines times for us to *stop* rather than *step*. When that happens, it may very well look and feel like '*a lack of progress*' or '*stagnation*' or '*laziness*' or '*failure*'. But maybe He values *stops* just as much, or more than *steps*. What is one to do when *God watches over your stops*?

You can probably guess how relevant this is to me, since, in many areas of my regular life God has determined a *stop*. Don't get me wrong, in many other ways, He is graciously allowing me *steps*. And I'm trying to relish those *steps*, whether they are well-worn routines or new *steps*. But it's the *stops* that get to us. For me, the *stops* are mostly related to retreat ministry and the many opportunities I crossed off my calendar for this summer and fall — people I didn't get to meet and places I didn't get to go — that ministry came to a *stop*.

Maybe you are experiencing a *stop* — or have experienced a *stop* in the past. God determines many *stops* for us. Newborns create a *stop*, injury from accidents produce a *stop*, personal illnesses, tragedies, economic downturns, effects of the irresponsibility of others — all of these and more can produce a *stop* — which I can guarantee you is *watched over by the Lord*.

I want to share a life-changing *stop* that happened to a well-known missionary. I have loved the life story of Amy Carmichael for decades. When I taught Sunday School, I used a multi-part, cliff-hanger story series on her life and I loved telling it so much. But now that I am the age she was when her major life-changing *stop* happened, the story takes on new significance.

If you don't know the story of Amy's missionary service in India, I'll give you a very brief summary. Before the turn of the previous century, she made an application with the China Inland Mission and was denied participation. After a short trial-start in Japan, Amy finally left to minister in India around age 25. Over time, the Lord opened her eyes to the plight of exploited children who were either given as an offering or outright sold to the temples of the Hindu gods — to be *married* to the gods — and live out a life of temple prostitution. Amy started a home for these vulnerable children called **Dohnavur Fellowship**. Over 1,000 children were rescued and educated and raised through her ministry.

Amy was a serious follower of Jesus. She was also serious about hard work. If she had been blessed with a smart watch in those days, she probably would have fallen into bed each night with 15,000+ *steps*. In fact, she had earned the nickname *hare* because of her active lifestyle and her uncanny ability to dash around from one task to another. The Lord truly directed her *steps,* until one day He directed her *stops.*

In October of 1931, at the age of 63, Amy went to inspect the construction site for their new hospital at the Fellowship. She fell into an uncovered pit, breaking her leg and twisting her spine. Medical efforts failed to restore her to full mobility, so for the last 20 years of her life, she was not able to live up to her nickname. She spent those years in her bedroom. She had *stopped* — But God's work had not *stopped* through her.

As her story goes, those last 20 years were some of the most fruitful and far-reaching of her entire life. Not only did she continue to direct the affairs of Dohnavur Fellowship, with its nurseries, homes, school, and hospital; but God used her accident in a way even Amy couldn't have expected. She wrote and published nearly 40 books which were a mixture of devotional writing and poetry which has been a great gift to the church up to this day. She also published a detailed account of the actual exploitation of children in India, uncovering a wicked practice. The impact of these books spread far beyond the thousands of rescued children — in fact, because of her writing, in 1948 child prostitution was outlawed in India.

God used Amy's accident in a way even Amy couldn't have expected — but she accepted God's plan — and that made all the difference. God guides our *steps,* and

He guides our *stops*. It is our privilege and responsibility to accept those *stops* and make the most of them.

As for me, I don't expect this season of *stopping* to last long — certainly nothing like Amy's situation — but it is a *stop* nonetheless. And maybe for you, or your loved one, you are experiencing a similar *stop* of some type that needs to be embraced so that God can make the best use of the season he has allowed in your life.

Smoke & Ashes

"Do not be conformed to this world, but be transformed by the renewal of your mind, that by testing you may discern what is the will of God, what is good and acceptable and perfect." Romans 12:2

We've had our share of smoke over the last few weeks here in Ontario. Actually, large portions of the country have been breathing the effects of summer wildfires. Some summers are worse than others for fire and smoke, and this one is in the *worse* category.

Most mornings I have a routine of heading out the back door to spruce up my patio for the day. I blow leaves off the deck and sometimes wipe down a spider web or two. I recently noticed that I also have to shake the accumulated white ash off my navy-blue chair cushions. They just sit there, minding their own business, and yet they get contaminated by these small particles that aren't really easy to detect until you see the cumulative blanket effect on my nice cushions.

This reminds me of the condition of our **minds** — just sitting there, *minding* our own business, our minds tend to get contaminated by the influences descending upon them. It's not always easy to detect the individual influence over our minds until we see the cumulative effect.

The Apostle Paul knew this, and prompted by the Holy Spirit, gave us a simple daily remedy to *shake off* the contamination. That's what our opening verse is talking about — being *transformed by the renewal of our mind.* This isn't a mysterious or complicated process. It's quite simple, like shaking the ash off my navy chair cushions. It just needs to be done regularly, or it will get increasingly worse.

What type of *ash* accumulates in our minds? All sorts of things that originate from inside our own head or come in through the front door — dissatisfaction with our current tasks in life, frustration with the political climate of our country, an unhealthy or destructive tendency to compare ourselves against others, the list is endless.

What does *renewal* look like? It's really not too different than *shaking out* patio cushions. Once we realize and admit there is a layer of unhelpful junk that has settled over our mind, and once we realize something should be done about that layer, we're in a position to begin the process of *renewal*. The best way to transform our minds is the consumption of the Word of God, which does the *shaking* work for us.

Hebrews 4:12 tells us —

> *"For the word of God is living and active, sharper than any two-edged sword, piercing even to the dividing of soul and spirit, of both joints and marrow, and quick to discern the thoughts and intents of the heart."*

Obviously, there is more to the *shaking out* process than just reading words on a page. We also have to receive what is being revealed, repent of what needs to go, and act upon what is good and useful and healthy.

What is the *result*? The Romans passage tells us that one of the most useful results is **discernment** — The ability to know what God's will is for today and for the future. Another result, which I personally crave is **peace**! **Isaiah 26:3** says,

> *"You will keep him in perfect peace, whose mind is stayed on you, because he trusts in you."*

Who doesn't want more peace in their life? Who doesn't aspire to move through life with a sense of contentment in whatever circumstances you're facing? It all begins with a little *shaking out*, just like I do daily to those ash-covered chair cushions. I'm going to remember what I've said here whenever I shake off those chair pads. My health issues invite a certain brand of *ash* to accumulate, and your life issues invite a different brand of *ash*. But we all need to busy ourselves with the *shaking* process.

How is Your Hearing?

"And your ears shall hear a word behind you, saying, "This is the way, walk in it," when you turn to the right or when you turn to the left."
Isaiah 30:21

During my walk last evening I noticed a steady stream of small planes in the sky. Our home is only two miles from our airport and we do see and hear planes occasionally, but recently it has been non-stop. Perhaps the fire season and the crop spraying season have converged. Maybe there are other reasons at play; but, whatever the case, it seems there are constantly planes in the sky lately.

While walking, I kept looking up to see what type of plane was following me and I couldn't help but remember when one of our tiny grandsons was fascinated with airplanes — and I mean fascinated! He could spot one in the sky well before any of us heard it or noticed it. He called them something that sounded like '*hair-pen*' which is only adorable to grandparents. And, as grandparents do, we immediately abandoned the perfectly acceptable English word for 'airplane' and proclaim, '*look, a hair-pen!*'

We parents and grandparents are a pitiful lot — embracing those charming made-up words and leaving behind everything we once held true and reasonable to cling to a new vocabulary crafted by an 18-month-old. You're smiling because you know full well you've done it too! How many words and actions and foods have been re-named in your household by little people? Worse, you've clung to the alternate pronunciation for years — decades! Paul and I have had an empty nest for a solid ten years and yet often use some of those heirloom toddler vocabulary words in our daily conversations. Pitiful!

Parents do eventually correct the toddlers, as they should. But I got to thinking that the same thing can happen in our spiritual lives. We can be just like toddlers and *hear* something wrong, continue to *hear* it wrong, *speak* it to others wrong, and eventually *believe* it wrong. It's cute when an 18-month-old hears a word wrong, but it's no longer cute when an adult Christian *hears* **The Word of God** wrong.

We *hear* things all the time that sound similar to the truth. Things like: *God helps those who help themselves,* or *if God closes a door, He will open a window,* or *everything happens for a reason.* Shall we call these *hair-pens*? If we're not careful, we begin to actually repeat what we *hear* and even believe what we *hear*. Heaven help us, when our friends and family pick up our spiritual vocabulary and we create an echo chamber of wrong hearing and wrong thinking.

The point of all this is a reminder to check our hearing. How is your hearing? During Jesus's earthly ministry, he said multiple times, **"He who has ears to hear, let him hear."** (**Matthew 11:15**). Two thousand years later, we are so blessed to have easy access to all of Jesus' words and the entire Bible, which speaks truth into our lives. But we still need to *hear it correctly*!

The reality is that we're all tempted to hear what we want to hear especially when we have layers of stress, or difficulty, or upheaval, or conflict, or health problems in our lives. During those seasons we may be prone to act like toddlers and *hear* things a certain way, *"What's that you say? God will never give you more than you can handle?"* We think to ourselves, *"That fits my life right now, I'm going to repeat that one!"* What just happened? You created a *hair-pen*. Something you *heard* and want to believe even though it sounds a little different than anything you actually find in the Bible.

The truth of God's Word is stable and consistent — we can't just rename or rebrand our idea of who God is and how He relates to us in order to match our circumstances in life.

So, what are we to do to improve our *hearing*? I've thought of three things:

- **Gifted Teaching**: There is no substitute for being taught the Word of God on a regular basis by someone whom God has gifted to teach the Scriptures. If your church meets that criteria then you should go as much as you possibly can. If it does not, you may have some searching to do.

- **Personal Listening**: It's also important to *hear* for ourselves. Do you have a reading schedule to read/hear the Bible for yourself regularly? Added bonus points if you can be involved in a small group that studies verse-by-verse, so you have the opportunity to discuss what you've just heard.

- **Open Heart**: Lastly, *hearing* the Word of God without a previous bias is critical. My husband just taught on this recently and it really captured my thinking (QR code to the link below). We always need to come to Scripture for what it is saying, not to reinforce something we learned in childhood or read on a Facebook Meme.

The summary is that we want to *be the adult* and not *the toddler* in our spiritual communications! No *hair-pens* for us!

Strength to Strength

"Blessed are those whose strength is in you... As they go through the Valley of Baca they make it a place of springs... They go from strength to strength." Psalm 84:5-8

This is my birthday week and although Paul says he's not very good at presents, I disagree. He's learned over the years not to try to surprise me but rather to ask, *'would you like such-and-such?'* I guess I appreciate the involvement. Afterall, we like to do things together.

This year he had an idea for a garden fountain and we worked together to find just the right color and size. It's now happily installed in the garden just outside our front door so that we can enjoy it when we come and go. I love it and I think it's the perfect birthday present.

I don't recall ever setting a fountain in motion before, but now I understand the process with the hidden pump, the tubing, and the reservoir. This particular fountain has three tiers, so it looks like the water is effortlessly flowing from the small bowl on the top, down to the next one, and ultimately into the largest. Then secretly, behind the scenes, it's being recycled and pushed back up to the top.

Coincidentally, my Bible reading this week was **Psalm 84** which was about water as well — *springs* and *pools*. Having recently been fiddling with my new water fountain, I may have read with a bit more interest.

Here is the full text to **Psalm 84:5-7 —**

> *"Blessed are those whose strength is in you, in whose heart are the highways to Zion. As they go through the Valley of Baca they make it a place of springs; the early rain also covers it with pools. They go from strength to strength; each one appears before God in Zion."*

Two things caught my attention:

#1 where these people's strength came from,

#2 the transformative effect these people had on the place they traveled through.

First of all, this Psalm is really about a pilgrimage of the ancient Hebrews to Jerusalem. Along the way they had to travel through a difficult place called the **Valley of Baca**. This valley was obviously a waterless wilderness, but their presence through the difficulty turned it into a *place of springs*. I am intrigued by the idea that you and I can travel through a dry and/or difficult place in our lives and leave that place so much better than we found it — we can have a *transformative effect* on the people in the difficult places we travel through.

Are you the type of person who *lights up a room*? I've never thought of myself that way and maybe you don't think you have the right personality for that. We might not. But, if we possess the light of Christ, we *do* have the potential to significantly change any place we travel through. The next time you lament how difficult your path may be (your *Valley of Baca*), you might consider that you have a distinct purpose in that valley to turn that dry wilderness spot into a place of refreshment for others. But *how,* you might ask. That's where the word *strength* comes into play (which is mentioned three times in these three verses).

The Psalmist blessed these people with that statement, **Blessed are those whose strength is in you.** Their strength was in the Lord — not in themselves. Here comes the link with my three-tiered fountain. If I relied only on the water in the upper urn flowing down to the next bowl, my fountain would last about seven and a half seconds.

BUT, with the strength of the hidden pump, water is continually moving back to the top to refill that urn and spill out to the next urn and the next to **make it a place of springs.**

The obvious reality that I've been contemplating is my reliance on the strength of the Lord as opposed to my reliance on that little bit of resource I possess in myself (represented by the water in the upper bowl)! Relying on God's strength doesn't happen automatically — even Christians can chose to rely on their own strength — we can chose to leave the power to the pump switched *off*.

You might consider this mental picture as well this week, and in your conversations with the Lord, ask Him to power that spiritual pump system in your life that allows His abundance of *living water* to flow through you. The Psalmist describes it as **going from strength to strength** so that you can transform a dry and difficult place into a **place of springs.**

Here are a few verses on the **strength of the Lord** that you might also appreciate:

> *Seek the LORD and his <u>strength</u>; seek his presence continually!* **(1 Chronicles 16:11)**

It is God who arms me with <u>strength</u>, and makes my way perfect. He makes my feet like the feet of deer, and sets me on my high place. **(Psalm 18:32-33 NIV84)**

I can do all things through him who <u>strengthens</u> me **(Philippians 4:13)**

I really do hope, in some small way, that as I travel through my own Valley of Baca the result may be a place of springs! And I hope the same for you as well.

Grace

"God is able to make all grace abound to you, so that having all sufficiency in all things at all times, you may abound in every good work."
2 Corinthians 9:8

We have six women who have been *born into* our family as daughters or grand-daughters. Three of them have the middle name of **Grace** — that's right — half of our female progeny share the same middle name. That makes it a very special name for us.

Grace is just an all-around fantastic word. It's useful in so many ways. It can mean beauty and elegance — like a ballerina. It can denote charm and poise in a person — think *Grace Kelly*. Then there are the actions of thankfulness and blessing — as in *saying grace*.

Additionally, in our spiritual vocabulary, we often define *grace* as *'unmerited favor'*. It means receiving from God something we don't deserve. We do not deserve, and neither can we earn God's forgiveness or a place within His family. Yet it is His *grace*, through faith, that opens the door for both those blessings. Do you see what a fantastic word it is?

But there is yet another application of the word *grace* that is at play in our focus passage today — the empowering work of God in our lives to *do* something, or to *endure* something, or to *share* something, or to *live through* something. Have you ever looked at someone else's very difficult situation in life and said to yourself, *I could never do that*? The truth is, you're right, you couldn't do that unless God's *grace* was given to you for that situation. That's what we call *grace that enables us to do*.

In our lives, God allows us to walk through situations where we desperately need *His grace* in order to not only survive, but also to *abound*. That's what the Apostle Paul was talking about in the verse I quoted above — God is able to make His grace *abound to us,* so we can turn around and *abound in every good work*. I have observed that it is in these seasons that we sometimes experience the most fruitfulness. This is the practical and helpful use of the word *grace*.

Think about your own life for a moment:

- What challenges are you facing that require

God's grace?

- Are you already aware of God's grace operating in your life?

- If you're walking through something difficult, have you asked for God's grace to *abound* toward you?

I think this verse written to the Corinthians can be snatched from its passage as a promise of sorts — right along with **Philippians 4:13** *"I can do all things through him who strengthens me."* God has not always promised to give us answers, but He has always promised to give us grace! Give it a try — let God's *grace* abound in your life!

Planted on Purpose

"Only let each person lead the life that the Lord has assigned to him, and to which God has called him." 1 Corinthians 7:17

I really love the end-of-August vibe. Most families have begun a back-to-school structure that usually has a calming effect. Most of the summer heat has subsided, and we're relieved to say good-bye to triple digits. Most of the mornings have that glorious crisp feel that we've been craving since the Fourth of July, and a cup of coffee on the porch returns to the wake-up routine.

Another thing I love about the end of August is the produce! I have some expert gardeners in my family, and I love those texts asking if I'd like some of their bounty. The garden table at our church is also a happy place right about now — I love to snatch some peppers or cucumbers that someone grew with care and decided to share.

A successful garden doesn't just happen on its own. A successful garden is planned, and each square foot is purposefully assigned to some variety of vegetable or fruit in order to give it the best opportunity to reach its full potential. The same is true with our spiritual lives. God is a master gardener, and although we usually think we're making all of our own decisions, God is planting His people in the perfect spot to reach their full potential.

Look at this verse from the Apostle Paul's speech on Mars Hill in Athens:

> *"From one man he made every nation of men, that they should inhabit the whole earth; and he determined the times set for them and the exact places where they should live."* **(Acts 17:26 NIV)**

Do you ever stop to consider that God planted you right where you are? That He placed you right in *this* time that you're living? You could have been planted anywhere else on the world's timeline, but God determined that you should live right here, right now. God is purposeful in his planting.

King David understood God's calling on his life for the time that *he* was planted in. Earlier in the book of Acts, Paul explained this,

> *"For when David had served God's purpose in his own generation, he fell asleep; he was buried with his fathers."* (**Acts 13:36**)

It inspires me to read that David *served God's purpose in his own generation.* If David served a purpose, so can I, and so can you! Serving God's purpose gives even more dimension to our theme verse about *the life assigned to us.* The point of this life assigned to us is to serve God's purpose.

In the same way that we have such a vast array of produce that originates from the same garden space, we have so many different purposes that have been assigned to us in the very time and place that we're living. Some of you are reading this from my own community; but some are reading from another country, even another continent. You're not floating through life without purpose. God has planted you on purpose so that you can fulfill His purpose in your own generation.

Here is one final thought on how we serve God's purpose from **Philippians 2:13** —

"It is God who works in you to will and to act according to his good purpose."

So, the happy summary is that 1) God has planted you on purpose, 2) He is the one who works in you to fulfill that purpose. All you have to do is yield to His work and be faithful regardless of the challenges or difficulties that you face.

Perspective

"For God has made me fruitful in the land of my affliction." Genesis 41:52

My yearly Bible reading plan runs from August to August (birthday to birthday), so I just finished Genesis this week. The life of Joseph is one of my favorite parts of that book. The way I see it, Joseph's character was mostly impeccable throughout his life. I suppose he could have been a bit more winsome in sharing his dream about his entire family bowing down to him — but he was, after all, a teenager and I keep a few pass cards at the ready for young men in that season of life.

Joseph earns points in my book for how he just kept rolling through the multiple injustices that came his way! First, the cruel rejection of his brothers (**Genesis 37**) must have been a trial of monumental proportions in his young life. Just imagine being sold by your own brothers! Yet, once sold as a slave in Egypt to Potiphar, he proved himself so useful that even Potiphar attested **that the Lord was with him (Genesis 39:3)**.

Then came the false sexual abuse accusation from Potiphar's wife, which landed Joseph in prison. But again, he landed on his feet. **Genesis 39:21** says,

> *"But the LORD was with Joseph and showed him steadfast love and gave him favor in the sight of the keeper of the prison."*

That *favor* basically meant that Joseph became the overseer of all of the prisoners, even though he was himself a captive.

A third major disappointment closed in on him after he accurately interpreted two dreams from two of his fellow prisoners. The chief baker was released and executed (as predicted), and the chief cup-bearer was restored to his position, just as Joseph had interpreted from his dream. However, rather than mentioning Joseph's plight to Pharoah, the cupbearer forgot all about him — FOR TWO MORE YEARS!

Those were three sizable afflictions in Joseph's life. We would describe him as someone who just *couldn't seem to catch a break* — and yet, Joseph continued to display patience and perseverance and hopefulness in the midst of his afflictions.

After those final two years in prison, when Pharaoh was in need of an interpreter-of-dreams himself, the chief cupbearer's memory returned. He told Pharaoh that *he once knew a guy in prison* who had the exact skill set required. Joseph proved useful, was finally released and began a new life *again,* this time serving at the highest level of Egyptian government.

Obviously, there is much more to the story, but eventually He was given a wife who bore him two sons and this whole devotion is inspired by the name that Joseph gave to his second son. Look at what came out of his mouth:

> **The name of the second he called Ephraim, "For God has made me fruitful in the land of my affliction." (Genesis 41:52)**

I read that phrase this week and had to put my Bible down and sit and think for a bit. After a decade of trials, Joseph could still see the hand of God doing good things in his life. This type of perspective doesn't come automatically to everyone. It is a choice to see life through the lens of gloom and doom, *or* to see the good things God is doing in our lives *even in the land of our afflictions.*

Joseph's choice to see God's hand working in his life had become a life-long habit. In fact, even after his father Jacob died, Joseph was able to tell his brothers,

> ***"As for you, you meant evil against me, but God meant it for good, to bring it about that many people should be kept alive, as they are today."*** **(Genesis 50:20)**

Maybe you are inspired along with me by Joseph's attitude. Most of us face a *land of affliction* at some point in our lives — or at several points in our lives. Being able to say **God has made me fruitful in the land of my affliction** can make the difference between a happy and hopeful life or a gloomy and glum life.

God's Hidden Hand

"See, I am doing a new thing! Now it springs up; do you not perceive it? I am making a way in the wilderness and streams in the wasteland."
Isaiah 43:19 (NIV)

Our family just enjoyed a wedding weekend filled with good food, cute little kids, a gorgeous bride, all the customary emotions, and all the fatigue! The next day we said a final *goodbye* to our girl who will be settling into the life of a military wife on the opposite coast. This is a whole new experience for us. So, as I write, if you are expecting an introspective piece about marriage or family or emotions you might be disappointed — or maybe relieved — depending on what you like to read.

What is actually on my mind is a little bit of wedding advice that recently came across my path. Someone had polled hundreds of wedding guests and discovered that the number one gift that a wedding couple can give back to their invited guests is to shorten the number of minutes between ceremony and food to single digits. Apparently, once the Mr. & Mrs. are pronounced, wedding guests are suddenly famished and start looking around for food!

In our case, I knew that Alyssa and John had planned for the feasting to begin immediately, and it did! They were barely down the grassy isle and the announcement was made as to where the dinner line would form. Here is where this is all going — before and during the ceremony, I hadn't been even vaguely aware of the caterer setting up the dinner, even though the serving tables were arranged only fifty feet away. The catering ladies had come on the property with such stealth and worked in the shadows of the porch so silently, that when the announcement was made, my inner wedding coordinator alarms went off. The first thing I did was look in the direction where I knew the dinner would be staged with the fear of seeing empty tables. But, NO! Everything was hot and ready, having been silently prepared for us in plain sight, but completely without our notice.

Speaking of working unnoticed, the subtitle of our Bible Study on the book of Esther is *When God Works in the Shadows*. I don't mean to be intentionally irreverent by drawing a parallel between the work the catering ladies did this weekend and the work that God does in our lives, but sometimes those simple analogies just hit the spot.

Maybe you've gone through a season where you just didn't *feel* God's presence in your life. Maybe you felt quite alone, as if God was extraordinarily distant. Maybe you worried about a great many things, believing you would glance over your shoulder only to find *empty tables* that would confirm your greatest fears that God had indeed left you to yourself — no longer interested or involved in your life. Maybe you feel all these things right now!

During the time of Esther, the Hebrew nation had been carried into exile and had lost so much — their land — their place of worship — even their identity as they were integrated into other nations. For the most part, I'm sure they didn't *feel* God's presence in their lives. To confirm this general sense, it's noteworthy that the name of God isn't even mentioned in the book of Esther. But just like the stealthy caterers working on the covered patio, God was there, setting things up and orchestrating people, places, and events for the benefit of His beloved.

In our lives, we often don't see or appreciate the hidden hand of God until we look back with perspective. That is when we understand the work He has actually done on our behalf. Acknowledging and celebrating what God has done in the shadows of our lives helps our faith to flourish in the present as we realize that God is always working, even when we can't (or won't) see Him, or notice Him, or *feel* His presence.

I can already look back with perspective after five months of treatment and see how God has been silently arranging things in my life to show his steadfast love toward me. And I can certainly look back with perspective over the decades of my life and see an even bigger picture of what God was doing all along to arrange things in my life.

Maybe you would benefit from pondering the hidden hand of God in your own life in the recent past as well as the distant past. You may find that it's a real faith booster!

A New Position

"So when the king's order was proclaimed...Esther also was taken into the king's palace and put in custody of Hegai, who had charge of the women." Esther 2:8

Do you enjoy a good football game? Most of the time I would say that I do — although sometimes I enjoy the good nap that happens during the good football game. Since Paul and I were both born in Minnesota we really have no choice in team loyalty — as Paul says, we were born with the Vikings tattoo. Rarely do they play well through the entire season, but somehow, we just keep watching. Maybe this will be their year!

Each player on a football team knows exactly what their position is and why they are there. This is no surprise to them. Sometimes players know their position from middle school on up. They're usually hired for their position. This is how football works. This is NOT how our spiritual lives work.

I'm thinking about Esther again this week. In a matter of ten short verses in *chapter two*, a young Jewish girl — Hadassah by her Hebrew name, Esther by her Persian name — went from being an orphaned trophy of war to the Queen of Persia. Talk about a change in position! There was nothing in *her* middle school years that could have prepared her for that position in life.

As we move on to *chapter three*, the significance of Esther's access to the King of Persia becomes clear — but that's not yet the case in chapter two. It just seems like a random, but fortunate turn-of-events.

This causes us to consider the position we find ourselves in right now in life. Maybe you can relate to the NFL quarterback, maybe from middle school until now God has placed you right where you always expected Him to place you. But maybe you're like the rest of us — you're often perplexed as to why you are where you are, why you are doing what you are doing, how you got to this place anyway. You're in a *chapter two* position, where you don't really understand the significance of where God has placed you and you may even wonder if you've made a wrong turn somewhere.

If that resonates with you, I'd like to offer a couple of thoughts.

- Sometimes God allows turns-of-events toward the positive, like Esther's experience; and sometimes toward the negative like, for example, Corrie ten Boom's experience. Both positive and negative placements can be God working behind the scenes of our lives.

- Our *chapter two* experiences in life can be short or long — what I mean is, the length of time that goes by until we perceive the significance of *why* God has put us into the position He has, can be quite short or very long.

- The best thing we can do while living out the position in which God has placed us is to be faithful regardless of if we like our current position or not.

We need to trust in the truthfulness of **Romans 8:28** —

"And we know that for those who love God all things work together for good, for those who are called according to his purpose."

Today I'm grateful that God faithfully moves us from one chapter to the next in our lives and that He *does* often reveal His plan.

Mixed Signals

The heart is deceitful above all things and beyond cure. Who can understand it? Jeremiah 17:9

I don't usually lead off with thoughts related to my treatments or physical situation — I'm way too private for all of that. However, a conversation was had this week, and I knew immediately that it should be the subject of my writing. Here is how it happened.

The chemotherapy I've had this summer has left me with some annoying neuropathy in my hands and feet. Often, as we crawl into bed at night, I apologize to my husband for my *cold* feet. The other night I even asked him if he would warm them up from their *frost-bitten* state. He grabbed ahold of my feet and smiled and said, "*Honey your feet are just as warm as the rest of your body. Your nerves are sending you wrong signals — you just can't trust them right now."* My **mouth** said something like, *"No, my toes are falling off, you need to hold them!"* But my **mind** knew he was completely right and right about far more than just the nerves in my feet.

We receive so many signals every day — some can be trusted, but many cannot. We send and receive signals in our relationships daily and often misinterpret those signals. If our spouse is silent, we may take it personally. If a co-worker is more direct than usual, we wonder what we did wrong rather than wonder what might have frustrated their day. These mixed-up signals cause us all kinds of problems.

But there are other relational *signals* in life that carry a bigger threat. Those are the signals related to how we interact with and understand the heart of God. We can easily misinterpret our circumstances to be an indicator of God's love for us — this gets us into big trouble and can severely damage our faith.

The nation of Israel completely mis-read their circumstances as they were traveling through the Wilderness on their way to the land God promised them.

Moses recounted this in Deuteronomy:

> *You grumbled in your tents and said, "The LORD hates us; so he brought us out of Egypt to deliver us into the hands of the Amorites to destroy us."* **(Deuteronomy 1:27)**

Isn't that just what we do? We find ourselves in a challenging circumstance and mis-read the whole episode! We think perhaps *God is punishing us — or brought this into our lives because He's disappointed in us.* Or we convince ourselves that *God has given up on us and has lost interest in protecting us.*

That is exactly how Israel read their situation — but, just like my own assessment of my toes — they were 100% wrong. Here is a passage later in Deuteronomy that expresses the reality of what was going on:

> *Because he loved your forefathers and chose their descendants after them, he brought you out of Egypt by his Presence and his great strength, to drive out before you nations greater and stronger than you and to bring you into their land to give it to you for your inheritance, as it is today.* **(Deuteronomy 4:37-38)**

Do you see the reality in those two passages? Israel interpreted as *hate* what God was doing out of *love*. Those are two opposites just like the *cold* and *hot* in my toes!

Back to that bed-time conversation — if I had simply checked out the reality of the situation by touching my feet rather than relying on how they *felt*, I would have known the truth. I would have been able to say, "*those slippery nerves are lying to me again tonight!*" And the same is true for our uncomfortable circumstances in life. If we would just check out the reality of the situation by consuming a steady diet of the Bible (God's love letter to us), rather than relying on how we *feel*, we would know the truth. The truth is that crummy circumstances happen to everyone, but God said He would never leave us or forsake us. Knowing the truth empowers us to press through a great many circumstances in life.

At Just the Right Time

Yet who knows whether you have come to the kingdom for such a time as this? Esther 4:14 (NKJV)

I'm thinking about Esther's life again this week — and those famous words listed above. Esther, whose Jewish heritage had been concealed, had randomly and unpredictably become the Queen of Persia. A short time later her entire race was slated for annihilation. It was actually Mordecai, her cousin, who posed the above question to her and we get the sense that both Mordecai and Esther simultaneously realized the truth of the rhetorical answer. Esther had indeed been placed within the palace *at just the right time* and God intended to use her presence there for His purposes — *if* she was willing to help others.

Have you ever experienced someone showing up in your life *at just the right time* to offer help? I remember Paul and I happening upon a terrible multi-car accident as we were returning from an event in Sun Valley years ago. It was not a heavily-trafficked road and we were only the fourth car on the scene, but as we stopped to see if we could help, wouldn't you know cars number one and two both contained trained medical people. What were the chances of those with the resources to help traveling on that lonely road *at just the right time*?

On another trip through the Badlands of South Dakota, we became the source of help that God put into position *at just the right time*. A cute little couple ran into big trouble with their too-low-to-the-ground sports car meeting up with too-high-above-the-ground rocks on the roads. (Pro-tip: sports cars and National Parks don't always play nicely together.)

Anyway, with a bounty of automotive fluids leaking, and a sliver of cell service, they were able to order a tow-truck from the nearest town — 90 miles away— that would arrive in about four hours. The remaining problem was waiting in 100+ degree temperatures, with no shelter or bathrooms, no food or water. But since *we* had seemingly been dispatched *for such a time as this*, we invited them into our trailer, started up the generator for some A/C, made a meal of pancakes and sausages, and the way I remember, the guy even took a shower in our trailer to wash off the auto diagnostics grime.

My Badlands story could hardly be compared to Esther's dramatic experience — no one's life was spared that hot day in South Dakota (that I know of). But I do wonder if all of us aren't placed in random and seemingly ordinary positions way more often than we're aware of to provide help and support — maybe simply comfort. Do we dare suggest that, like Esther, we're often placed *for such a time as this?* I think we can. My simple encouragement to all of us is to be more aware of how God might use us each day.

Here is a great passage from Ephesians that says in New Testament language what the story of Esther describes:

> *Be very careful, then, how you live — not as unwise but as wise, making the most of every opportunity, because the days are evil. Therefore do not be foolish, but understand what the Lord's will is.* **(Ephesians 5:15-17)**

Even on a normal day like today — who knows that you haven't been placed in just the right place at just the right time to carry out God's will.

Factory Reset

"...Blessed be the LORD, who has not left you this day without a redeemer... he shall be to you a restorer of life..." Ruth 4:14-15

For quite some time, Paul and I have been in the season of life where we pass along our cast-off cell phones to one of the grandkids. Recently however, we took advantage of a trade-in offer and that worked too. We performed the required *factory reset*, sent off the device, and received a substantial rebate.

Regardless of where your retired tech goes, *factory resets* are essential. For one thing, you don't want to pass along your personal information to the next owner; but also, devices begin to act sort of worn-down after years of use. Often a phone or laptop has simply experienced too much life, collected too much clutter, and it really needs to be wiped clean. Sometimes people also experience too much life, collect too many complications, operate with too much confusion, and begin to feel worn-down by everything that has happened — they need a *reset*.

This is how I see Naomi in the book of Ruth. From the opening verses, we learn that Naomi suffered through too much life, too much tragedy, and too much grief — she was no longer functioning at full capacity. It all started with a dramatic migration away from her home. Then came the death of her husband, followed by the unthinkable — the death of both of her sons. By the time she finally made her way back to Judah she was a shadow of her former self.

Ruth 1:19-20 tells us her friends no longer recognized her:

> ***The women said, "Is this Naomi?" She said to them, "Do not call me Naomi; call me Mara*** (which means *bitter*).

If there was ever a soul who needed a *factory reset* in order to function properly, it was Naomi.

Do you ever wish you could somehow do a *factory reset* on your life? Maybe you haven't experienced the drama that Naomi did, but you still sense you're just not functioning as well as you once did — as well as you could.

One of the nuggets of inspiration we acquire through the short book of Ruth is the amazing restoration of Naomi's life. Just read that theme verse at the beginning again — God took her from *no sons* and *bitterness,* to having a *grandson* who would be *a restorer of life.* That's what factory resets do — they restore things!

Naomi's *reset* didn't happen overnight; however, it wouldn't have happened at all if not for one important choice she made. **Ruth 2:7** tells us

> **"...she set out from the place where she was...and went on the way to return to the land of Judah."**

I've often paraphrased this verse as follows: *she pointed her feet in God's direction and started moving.*

As for us, whenever we feel we're not functioning as well as we could, the first critical step is to humble ourselves and point our feet in God's direction. I believe He will respond and begin that process of restoration in our lives. It might not be an overnight change — but God is in the business of *restoring,* and step-by-step He is a *restorer of life* for us.

Why Not Me?

If one part of the body suffers, all the parts suffer with it. 1 Corinthians 12:26

I'm quite sure most of you spent a good amount of time in the recent weeks following the saga of those two back-to-back hurricanes, Helene and Milton. Natural disasters aren't new —we've always experienced wildfires, tornadoes, hurricanes, and earthquakes and people have always been affected by these disasters.

But what I'm pondering this week is the effect that other people's suffering has on me (and you). The flooded communities in North Carolina are a good example. I see photos or watch videos and feel a strange tug in my heart that asks, *why them and why not me?* Why am I safe and happy and warm and dry and grocery shopping and going to a ball game and sleeping in my comfortable bed tonight? The untouched normalcy of my life produces a sort of mis-placed sense of guilt — yet, I have nothing to be guilty about, so it must be grief.

I'm sure you have also been distraught when you hear of losses from a distance, and I'm sure your heart hurts for people closer to home who are suffering in all sorts of seen and unseen ways. It doesn't have to be a huge natural disaster for people to suffer — couples struggle in their marriage, parents suffer when their children go rogue, families have financial crises, friends suffer from health problems.

God designed us to live in community to the extent that we carry each other's burdens, so it does come naturally for us to empathize with the suffering of others. The Apostle Paul described Christians, as being **knit together in love** (**Colossians 2:2**). Our theme verse reminds us *if one part of the body suffers, all the parts suffer with it* (**1 Corinthians 12:26**).

But here is the balance — we also live in a world of rejoicing! Babies are being born, couples are getting married, contracts are being signed, preschoolers are learning to do chores! For all of the **suffering** around us there is an equal portion of **rejoicing** and **Romans 12:15** charges us to *rejoice with those who rejoice and weep with those who weep.*

Are you up for the task of doing both at the same time — extending sympathy and handing out attaboys in the same hour? The truth is that other people will sometimes suffer when our life is smooth, and we will sometimes suffer when their lives are smooth. So, let's do whatever we can to weep with those who weep (even if it's as impersonal as sending relief funds to flood victims), and let's rejoice with those who aren't currently suffering — they need our support as well. Mark my words, we will all take our turn at both suffering and rejoicing throughout our lifetime, so let's do it together!

I really have been on the receiving end of so much love. So many have stopped for a moment to enter my world and send a card, give a hug, offer a word of encouragement, and to pray. I feel that I've been in a classroom with hundreds of instructors who have taught me well the concept of *carrying one another's burdens*.

The Power of Boredom

"So teach us to number our days that we may get a heart of wisdom." Psalm 90:2

Have the words "I'm bored" ever come out of your mouth? In general, I don't mind an under-programmed day at all, so I can't recall declaring a sense of boredom very often in my life, but I suppose it's been there.

I grew up in blizzard country. The technology for accurately predicting weather was still a few decades from being perfected, so a snowstorm could easily creep up right in the middle of the school day when I was young. Since it would be too dangerous for the buses to shuttle us back to our homes in the country, we would be *stuck* in town — for who knows how long. My mother's sister lived right next to the school, so I always knew exactly where I would be spending the night when a blizzard stirred up trouble. Sometimes it was a couple of nights!

My Aunt Linda was a minimalist before it was popular. Her home was tidy and other than a robust plant collection it was somewhat bare. In mid-west homes the basement was almost always the designated space for children to *play*. But when you descended the wooden stairs in Aunt Linda's house, you would find an abundance of concrete and a scarcity of toys, or books, or really anything much for children. In all fairness to her, her own children had grown and left home many years earlier.

But the strange sensation that I remember in her home and even in her basement was one of peace. Maybe that only means that I'm a *minimalist* as well. Or maybe it means that I never really minded being alone with my thoughts or coming up with creative possibilities when there wasn't much in the way of alternatives.

The point I'm building up to is the *power of boredom* — maybe we should call it the *hidden blessing of boredom.*

What some might consider a *boring* situation often carries great potential. Look what it did for King David in his early years of tending his father's sheep. There had to have been precious few avenues of entertainment and an abundance of time to ponder things greater than himself. David was able to spend long evenings studying the stars. He learned to serenade his sheep with his harp and develop lyrics of praise to God. He must have crafted slings, gathered stones, and practiced endlessly — until he was proficient enough to kill a lion or a bear (**1 Samuel 17:34-35**).

David had as much grass as Aunt Linda had concrete — and not much else. But look what he did with his *boring* circumstances! He used it to a great advantage, as have many other great thinkers and inventors and artists and theologians and regular Christians. Oh, that we had more scarcity and less busy-ness in our lives — I wonder what we might accomplish for God's Kingdom.

You may find yourself recently in situations which you consider *repetitive* or *boring*. Maybe this is a new experience for you. Perhaps this simple phrase — *the power of boredom* — might cause you to view your situation differently and inspire you to ponder things greater than yourself. Perhaps God is actually giving you a gift by removing distractions in order to develop other significant areas of your life to better serve Him.

Maybe some of this conversation is what is at the heart of our theme verse: ***So teach us to number our days that we may get a heart of wisdom.***

Incremental Healing

Then Jesus laid his hands on his eyes again; and he opened his eyes, his sight was restored, and he saw everything clearly. Mark 8:25

At some point in your life, you've probably struggled to maintain your passion to finish a project. Along came a well-meaning Sally Sunshine and reminded you that, "*Rome wasn't built in a day.*" You may have smiled on the outside, perhaps even thanked them for the great reminder, but on the inside, you were tired and just wanted it to be that day when Rome *was actually* finished.

Some projects just take time — even though we would rather have instant results. As I was reading the gospel of Mark today, I noticed an interesting thing about someone who came to Jesus for healing — the healing took some time. All of the previous healing encounters were instant, but here came this blind man and Jesus healed him incrementally. Here's how the passage reads, from **Mark 8:23-25**:

> *And he took the blind man by the hand and led him out of the village, and when he had spit on his eyes and laid his hands on him, he asked him, "Do you see anything?" And he looked up and said, "I see people, but they look like trees, walking." Then Jesus laid his hands on his eyes again; and he opened his eyes, his sight was restored, and he saw everything clearly.*

That was a new twist in the long list of healings Jesus had performed up to that point — healing in two stages. I'm not going to comment from a theological perspective (since I'm not one), but I'd like to comment from a personal perspective. Here are all the things I love about *how* this blind man was incrementally healed and what it could mean for me:

- If I come to the Lord asking for healing and I don't receive all that I've asked for, I have permission to be honest and say so — I can admit it's not perfect.

- The implication is that I can be thankful for what I *have* received, even if it's not 100% complete.

- The implication is that I can ask for more healing.

- The underlying message from this encounter is a reminder about patient perseverance rather than a reliance on instantaneous results.

I know this blind man's incremental healing was a minority experience in the Gospels. But in our lives, don't you feel that incremental healing is a majority experience? How often have you prayed for healing or restoration and had to apply patient perseverance way more often than you've enjoyed instant results?

What is your prayer request right now? Are you asking for the restoration of a relationship? Incremental restoration is a win — keep asking! Are you asking for physical healing? Incremental healing is a real experience — thank the Lord for what he *has* done and be honest about your further needs.

How does this relate to me? Well, I do feel that God has been present in my treatments thus far to offer incremental healing. However, I can identify with the blind man when he was honest about his sight — it wasn't great yet. If I were to be honest, I would say that I feel my cancer is very likely under control, but I'd like further healing from some of the side-effects that have plagued me. I'll just apply some patient perseverance to this request!

Yet, I Will Rejoice

"... yet I will rejoice in the LORD; I will take joy in the God of my salvation." Habakkuk 3:18

Have you ever caught yourself telling God how to run the world? Maybe you haven't actually spoken the instructions to Him or handed over an agenda, but we've all probably entertained the thought, 'God, *how could you let this happen?*'

I was doing a bit of cleaning in my living room the other day and found myself dusting off a really interesting wooden tray that I had commissioned my daughter to make about eight years ago for a women's retreat. As I took the books off the tray to wipe off the dust and crumbs, I re-read the hand-painted phrase, *"Yet I will rejoice!"* from Habakkuk chapter 3.

Our retreat theme that year was *Satisfied* and I taught from Habakkuk in the evening session. I opened my teaching this way, "*It's a crummy feeling to be saved, but not satisfied with how God is running the world.*" That pretty much describes how Habakkuk felt — he loved God, he was happy to know God, he lived among God's people, but in that moment of time he wasn't so sure that all of God's decisions were appropriate or even fair. He spent quite a little time asking questions of God like, 'Don't you care?' 'Why aren't you doing something about this?'

Those questions might sound familiar. We all have things in our world that aren't right, things that are unraveling, things that are in crisis mode. Even if we don't verbally ask, we think the same questions. But, if we were to summarize God's response to Habakkuk it would go something like this, "*Oh, I have a plan, I'm not without a plan, your world isn't running on its own track, I'm completely in control.*"

The blessing of this short book of the Bible is that it shows us how Habakkuk didn't simply accuse God and turn the other way. He was persistent with his questions — we would call it persevering in prayer today. He continued in prayer until he was able to see his world through the lens of God's perspective and he finally came to understand that his satisfaction wouldn't be found in everything being made whole and comfortable and prosperous, but rather in knowing that God is good and He is in control.

Look at the same conclusion that the Psalmist came to in **Psalm 145:17-19** —

> *"The LORD is righteous in all his ways and kind in all his works. The LORD is near to all who call on him, to all who call on him in truth. He fulfills the desire of those who fear him; he also hears their cry and saves them."*

Knowing these things is what enabled Habakkuk to burst into verse in **Habakkuk 3:17-18** —

> *"Though the fig tree should not blossom, nor fruit be on the vines, the produce of the olive fail and the fields yield no food, the flock be cut off from the fold and there be no herd in the stalls, yet I will rejoice in the LORD; I will take joy in the God of my salvation."*

In other words, I will rejoice in God even if things are not set right in my world, I know they will eventually be set right in God's time and in God's way. That is true satisfaction.

Distant

"Because you are his sons, God sent the Spirit of his Son into our hearts, the Spirit who calls out, "Abba, Father." Galatians 4:6

Just today I finished the draft of our women's verse-by-verse Bible study through the gospel of Mark. I've titled it *Following Jesus*. It's the first *full* gospel that we will have gone through in our Women of the Word Studies and I'm pretty excited about it.

Mark is the only gospel writer who recorded Jesus' prayer in the Garden of Gethsemane to begin with **"Abba Father" (Mark 14:36)** and I'm glad he did. Even in His distress, we catch a glimpse of Jesus' intimate relationship with His Father in Heaven.

Abba was an Aramaic word that Jewish children would have used to address their father — something like daddy or papa for us today. But the point is that it reflected a close and warm relationship.

The opposite of *close* would be *distant* so you may wonder why I titled this post with that single word. Well, the reason is that my husband's second book has recently been published and its title is, **"Why Do I Feel so Distant from God?"**

Does that resonate with you? Have you ever felt a sense of distance from God? I think we all have, because even the Psalmist said *"Why, O Lord, do you stand far away?"* (**Psalm 10:1**) That verse is actually the opening verse of Paul's book. (By the way, if this does resonate with you — feeling distant from God — I invite you to order a copy using the link at the end of this chapter. I think you will be blessed.

The bottom line is that God has always desired a *close* relationship with us, rather than a *distant* one. There are so many promises in Scripture that are intended to inspire us toward a close relationship with God, like the following:

> **Psalm 73:28 —** *But for me it is good to be near God; I have made the Lord God my refuge, that I may tell of all your works.*

John 15:15 — *No longer do I call you servants, for the servant does not know what his master is doing; but I have called you friends, for all that I have heard from my Father I have made known to you.*

John 15:9 — *As the Father has loved me, so have I loved you. Abide in my love.*

James 4:8 — *Draw near to God, and he will draw near to you.*

When we feel *distant*, it might help us to dwell on verses like these to restore that sense of a close relationship with the Lord.

Pastor Paul's Book Link

Come Away

"Come away by yourselves to a desolate place and rest a while." Mark 6:30

"Hey there!"

"Oh hi, good to see you!"

"You too. How's it been going?"

"Oh busy. I've been really busy!"

Does that sound like a grocery store interaction that's familiar to you? I suppose we don't really divulge all of our deepest dreams or disappointments over the tomato bin — we keep it fairly superficial. But how often do we describe our lives as *being busy*? We say that because it's true — we *are* busy!

Jesus and his disciples were busy too. In fact, one time they were described in the gospel of Mark as being so busy ministering to people that they didn't even have time to eat! Here is how the passage is actually worded:

> *"For many were coming and going, and they had no leisure even to eat."* (**Mark 6:31**)

When our four kids were all home and in different stages of life and activities from age 3 to 16, I was often too busy to even eat. I felt like **Mark 6:31** totally described my existence: *'for many were coming and going!'* But the funny thing is that busyness sometimes becomes addictive. Even when the kids are grown and gone, we're still busy. Why is that?

A lot of the things we're busy with are good things. Paul and I are busy with many projects, ideas, people, and responsibilities; and I bet you are too. Being busy isn't all bad.

But what I love about this interaction that Jesus had with his disciples is that He knew it was neither profitable nor healthy for them to sustain their busyness for long without some renewal. That's why He invited them to *"come away...and rest a while."* This is my simple encouragement for us as we are on the doorstep of the busiest time of the year — make time to *come away...and rest your soul.*

Matthew 11:28-30 is such a wonderful reminder and promise for renewal:

> *"Come to me, all who labor and are heavy laden, and I will give you rest. Take my yoke upon you, and learn from me, for I am gentle and lowly in heart, and you will find rest for your souls. For my yoke is easy, and my burden is light."*

It's far easier to write about or talk about than it is to actually set aside time to DO. But, if it was important for Jesus' disciples, I'm pretty sure it's important for us as well!

Give thanks in all Circumstances?

"Give thanks in all circumstances; for this is the will of God in Christ Jesus for you." 1 Thessalonians 5:18

"What are you grateful for?"

That was the usual Thanksgiving table talk when our children were young — honestly, it's still what we talk about at Thanksgiving. I'll bet many of your households are similar. Somehow passing a large bowl of perfectly mashed potatoes followed with homemade gravy makes it a little easier to recall what we're grateful for.

But there are many other moments both before and after that beautiful dinner on the table when it's not so easy to be thankful. Many of those moments are complicated — loved ones are missing from the gatherings — health challenges have taken their toll — relationships have deteriorated or broken completely — financial stability has teetered — or we're just plain tired and stressed. When any of those situations become real, our hearts hurt, and our minds are distant and it's a bit challenging to even figure out what there is to be thankful for.

The interesting thing about our theme verse from 1 Thessalonians is that the Apostle Paul charged his readers to *give thanks in ALL circumstances*. What he meant was to give thanks when the mashed potatoes were hot and buttery and perfect and also to give thanks when the eyes were swollen from tears and the heart ached. Because there truly *is* something to be grateful for in *every* circumstance.

That's one thing I've learned through this season of treatment. Whenever I had to be somewhere I didn't want to be, talk about things I didn't want to consider, do things I would rather not — there was *always* something to be thankful for. And even if I didn't find *something* to be thankful for, I could rest in *someone* to be thankful for because I always knew that my Lord was right with me.

Elisabeth Elliott once said, *"Let thanksgiving be the habit of your life."* I love that thought. When something becomes a habit — we just do it — we hardly think about it at all. I wonder if that isn't the key to *giving thanks in ALL circumstances*. And by the way, the Apostle Paul didn't say to give thanks *for* all circumstances, but rather, *in the midst* of those circumstances. However, I've learned in life that sometimes we turn around and even give thanks *for* the rough patches because of what the Lord did in our lives through them.

You don't have to wait for the Thanksgiving holiday to cultivate the habit of *thanks-giving*. Today is a perfect day to share some of what you are thankful for with someone in your life.

A Light has Dawned

"The people walking in darkness have seen a great light; on those living in the land of the shadow of death a light has dawned." Isaiah 9:2 (NIV84)

We usually set up our Christmas tree the weekend following Thanksgiving. I try really hard not to put up Christmas decorations before Thanksgiving to let that holiday have its unique place. I'll be honest, sometimes it takes a bit of self-control, especially in years like this one when Thanksgiving and Christmas are about as close together as they ever get. But it's up now, lit and decorated.

Christmas trees don't just blend into the living room space like a picture on the wall — they make a statement!

In fact, I always have to rearrange furniture a bit to accommodate the tree — I bet you do too. This weekend, once I struck the perfect re-arrangement, and the tree was lit, and the fireplace was on, I told Paul, "*I really love this cozied-in feeling.*" He said, "*Yeah, what exactly is a cozied-in feeling?*" "*Crowded.*" I replied, "*It's now Christmas crowded, and I love it!*"

Like I said, the Christmas tree doesn't simply blend in — it demands to be noticed. Of all the Christmas decorations we set out, I think the lighted Christmas tree is one of our best reminders that God sent His son to **bring light** into a dark world. Why is it the greatest reminder, you ask me? Well, think about it, trees come from a forest (well, mine actually came from Home Depot about 15 years ago, but just hang with me here) and forests are typically dark. So, the point is, we put something right into the center of our homes that represents a dark place but with a twist. We light it up to demonstrate that something has changed, something extraordinary has happened.

What is that extraordinary change? Well, that's what our theme verse prophesied — **that people walking in darkness have seen a great light.** The verse prior to this one pointed to a specific place (**v.1**) **... in the future he will honor Galilee of the Gentiles, by the Way of the Sea, beyond the Jordan.** The basic fulfillment of that prophecy was the light of Jesus' ministry in the area of Galilee. That's where about 80% of his ministry happened. But Galilee hasn't always had the corner on the darkness market — our world is dark too.

A dark world makes me think about Jesus' words in the Sermon on the Mount in **Matthew 5:14-16** —

> *"You are the light of the world. A city on a hill cannot be hidden. Neither do people light a lamp and put it under a bowl. Instead they put it on its stand, and it gives light to everyone in the house. In the same way, let your light shine before men, that they may see your good deeds and praise your Father in heaven."*

Christmas trees can't really be hidden, neither can cities on a hill or a lit lamp in a room — they *make a statement*. Jesus was telling his followers that *they* need to *make a statement* as well — not an obnoxious *'look at me'* statement, but a statement of hope!

Our light often shines the brightest when things in our personal world have darkened for some reason. If that is the case with you, then *let your light shine*.

A Catalog of Empathy

"Praise be to...the God of all comfort, who comforts us in all our troubles, so that we can comfort those in any trouble with the comfort we ourselves have received from God." 2 Corinthians 1:3-4 (NIV84)

A few years ago, Paul and I were enjoying Glacier National Park for an anniversary trip. We decided to elevate our vacation by running up to Waterton Park just over the border in Alberta, Canada for a few days. It was fantastic, and we would highly recommend it if you ever get the chance to head up there.

Fortunately, we had brought our passports and were met by a border crossing agent with personality — which was a plus! She noted that we had very few stamps in our passports and seemed genuinely pleased to add to our meager assortment.

Truth be told, I have always wanted to be that person with an abundance of stamps in my passport. You know, it sort of validates a girl to show how many countries you've been to. But the Lord hasn't really made me that kind of person. But He has been making a different kind of person with a different abundance of stamps that is actually much more useful.

One fine October morning this fall, while I was walking laps around the St. Luke's Hospital campus, waiting for my surgery check-in, the Lord spoke to me about abundance of a different type. He ministered to me that He had actually been adding stamps — not in my passport, but in my **Catalog of Empathy**. It was being filled up like the S&H green stamp books of old.

Empathy stamps help us relate to others' difficulties, and comfort others in their difficulties, like our theme verse states. We become much more effective because we have experienced similar difficulties ourselves and have received comfort from the Lord. We know the path.

Cancer, chemo, surgery, radiation, neuropathy, loss of nails, those are some of my *stamps* that were added in 2024 in my **Catalog of Empathy**. I had never aspired to any of those *stamps*, I had only been focused on *stamps* from interesting countries. But, at the end of the day, it's easy to see how much more useful these *empathy stamps* are, both in my own life and my usefulness to others.

Maybe you've collected a bunch of *stamps* in your **Catalog of Empathy** this past year. Maybe you didn't aspire to them either, but I hope you might now understand how valuable they are. Maybe you need to pull out your catalog and peruse all of those stamps and ask God how He wants to use them in your life. I promise you, they are more valuable than your full passport.

A Great Time for Friends

"Carry each other's burdens, and in this way you will fulfill the law of Christ." Galatians 6:2 (NIV84)

Do you sometimes wish you were more outgoing? Do you wish for a magical switch to boost your charisma in order to make friends more easily? Some of you actually *do* make friends quickly and easily. Our daughter says that she and her husband can go out to dinner and before the credit card has been swiped, he's made four new friends, two potential business deals, and received an offer to be a groomsman in someone's wedding. That may be stretching things a bit — but some of you collect friends as quickly as flies on your picnic lunch.

LEANING INTO THE PRESENCE OF THE LORD

I'm nothing like my son-in-law. I have to work hard to establish relationships, probably just like you do. But every once in a while, some great need comes along in our lives that reveals just how many friends we actually have — and how valuable those relationships are — and we are astonished. That happened to a man early on in Jesus' earthly ministry. His great need was that he was paralyzed, which is debilitating in any age, but in the first century it was particularly devastating.

But this man had friends. Friends that were invested in his life. Friends that were willing to step up and help. Friends that had heard about Jesus and believed He could help and heal. The short story is told this way in the Gospel of Mark:

> **Mark 2:3-5, 11-12** *And they came, bringing to him [Jesus] a paralytic carried by four men. And when they could not get near him because of the crowd, they removed the roof above him, and when they had made an opening, they let down the bed on which the paralytic lay. And when Jesus saw their faith, he said to the paralytic..."I say to you, rise, pick up your bed, and go home." And he rose and immediately picked up his bed and went out before them all, so that they were all amazed and glorified God.*

This man's friends were willing to not only *bring him to Jesus*, but they were willing to put in a bit of personal labor by hauling him up on the roof, dismantling it, and lowering him *right in front of Jesus!* That's quite a picture, isn't it? It's quite inspiring whether you are the one in need or the one with a friend in need.

I have been the one with *a friend in need* for the majority of my life, but this year I became the one in need. I have now experienced what it's like to have friends who will put in the effort to bring me *right in front of Jesus* through prayer. I have saved every single card and note that was sent to let me know you were praying. In fact, my box of cards was getting pretty full and I decided to put it on the bathroom scale one day — FIVE pounds of cards and letters!

Can you even imagine how encouraging that is to receive? And I know that each one represented someone with the same heart as the fellas in Mark's story — giving up their time and comfort to ask Jesus to heal their friend. And I believe He has done just that!

So, first, I want to say *thank you* from the bottom of my heart for being the kind of friend that would bring me to Jesus for healing. You have inspired me to be a better friend as well.

Next, I want to tell you that by the end of this week, I'll be completely finished with all three forms of treatments that were prescribed for me: chemotherapy, surgery, and radiation. Unlike other types of cancer that can reveal whether one is *cancer free* through blood work, I will simply need to move forward with my life *assuming* the cancer has been eradicated and follow the future surveillance schedule to confirm that.

Lastly, my journey has basically been 35 weeks long. I wrote the first devotion titled *'Leaning into the Presence of the Lord'* on April 24, 2024. On that day, crossing the finish line of treatment seemed very distant. And look — here I am — officially crossing in two more days!

Like the *paralytic*, mine is a relatively happy ending, but I'm keenly aware that everyone who reads this knows someone who wasn't healed of cancer. There can be an abundance of emotions that go along with even speaking the "C" word, and there can be a tendency to protect ourselves from further disappointment. This protection might cause us to shrink back from praying for ourselves or others. So, I think the most useful encouragement I can close with is to continue to *bring your friends right in front of Jesus* and let Him decide the outcome. God is good and he will always act in His time and His way.

My Love & Blessings,

Sue

***

"Thus says the LORD: "Let not the wise man boast in his wisdom, let not the mighty man boast in his might, let not the rich man boast in his riches, but let him who boasts boast in this, that he understands and knows me, that I am the LORD who practices steadfast love, justice, and righteousness in the earth. For in these things I delight, declares the LORD." **Jeremiah 9:23-24**

***

A granddaughter's graduation

Silly grandkids on Mother's Day

Our Anniversary

Snapshots OF MY Life

A lot of life happens within a thirty-five week window. The Lord enabled me to be present and enjoy all of that life. Here is a little peek...

Recording a Q&A for our channel

About the Author

Sue LeBoutillier has helped her husband (Paul) pastor a church in Ontario, Oregon for almost 35 years. They have four grown children who have brought three spouses and six grandchildren into their family.

Sue has enjoyed a fruitful retreat-speaking ministry both in the U.S. and internationally and published over twenty-five Bible studies through her Women of the Word ministry

Some of the most popular titles include:

— The Coming King (1 Samuel)

— Finding Purpose (Ephesians)

— While We Wait (Titus)

— Real Faith for Daily Life (James)

Her Bible studies and their accompanying videos can be found at www.lifebibleministry.com:

Printed in Dunstable, United Kingdom